C000000518

THE CUMBRIA CYCLE WAY

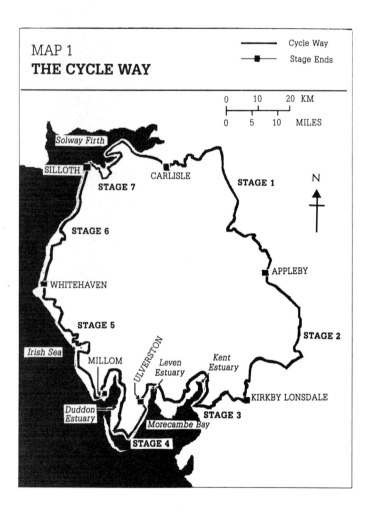

MAP 1
THE CYCLE WAY

— Cycle Way
■— Stage Ends

0   10   20   KM
0   5   10   MILES

Solway Firth
SILLOTH
CARLISLE
STAGE 7
STAGE 1
N
STAGE 6
APPLEBY
WHITEHAVEN
STAGE 2
STAGE 5
ULVERSTON
Irish Sea
MILLOM
Leven Estuary
Kent Estuary
Duddon Estuary
KIRKBY LONSDALE
STAGE 3
Morecambe Bay
STAGE 4

THE CUMBRIA CYCLE WAY

by

ROY WALKER & RON JARVIS

CICERONE PRESS
MILNTHORPE, CUMBRIA

© R.Walker and R.Jarvis, 1992
ISBN 1 85284 106 0

ACKNOWLEDGEMENTS

We thank the following for their assistance in preparing this book. The responsibility for errors and opinions expressed remains ours.

John Studholme of the Cumbria County Planning Department; Vicky Crossfield of Harden, Bingley, West Yorks for the use of her expertise in cycle touring; Alan Jarvis of Ponteland, Northumberland, for reading the manuscript and checking the proofs; Martin Rowe of Arnside, Cumbria, for the use of his darkroom, his time and his knowledge; The Manjushri Institute, Conishead Priory, Ulverston; VSEL (Vickers Shipbuilding & Engineering Ltd), Barrow-in-Furness; Ministry of Defence, Proof and Experimental Establishment, Eskmeals, Millom; BNFL (British Nuclear Fuels plc), Sellafield; Albright & Wilson, Whitehaven; and many members of the public all over the county who patiently answered our questions or helped us in other ways. And, finally, our wives, Anne and Mary, for their tolerance and assistance.

Advice to Readers

Readers are advised that whilst every effort is taken by the author to ensure the accuracy of this guidebook, changes can occur which may affect the contents. It is advisable to check locally on transport, accommodation, shops etc but even rights-of-way can be altered and, more especially overseas, paths can be eradicated by landslip, forest fires or changes of ownership.

The publisher would welcome notes of any such changes

Front Cover: Cyclists resting at Cartmel
Photo courtesy of Cumbria County Council

CONTENTS

*Mr Charles Ross, Chairman of the County Council, re-launches
the Cumbria Cycle Way at Talkin Tarn on May 1st, 1990*

INTRODUCTION

The Cumbria Cycle Way grew from an idea of the late Wesley Park, Recreation and Amenities Officer of Copeland District Council, Cumbria. It opened in 1980 and was the first of its kind in the United Kingdom. The route has since been improved and waymarked by the County Council, in consultation with the Cumbria Cycling Club, the District Councils and the Lake District and North Yorkshire Dales National Park authorities. Cumbria County Council has also produced a leaflet on the Cycle Way, which is obtainable from the County Planning Department and from tourist information offices. This book is intended to supplement the leaflet, not to replace it.

The Cycle Way is a carefully thought-out route, mostly along minor roads, extending 260 miles in a roughly circular shape (see Map 1). From Carlisle it follows the foot of the escarpment of the northern Pennines to Kirkby Stephen. From there it goes through valleys in the central Pennines as far as Kirkby Lonsdale and then reaches Morecambe Bay at Arnside. After winding around the sheltered recesses of the Bay and the Duddon Estuary it emerges on to the open coast of the Irish Sea. Eventually it reaches the quieter waters and salt marshes of the Solway Firth before returning to Carlisle. Cumbria is not noted for its seaside, yet more than half of the Cycle Way is near the coast. It also reaches 1500 feet above sea-level at the head of the Eden valley. Apart from the diversity of landscape there's also a great variety of towns: the cathedral city of Carlisle, historic market towns and no fewer than five towns established within the last two centuries.

You don't have to start at Carlisle, of course. Fortunately much of the route is near to a railway (see Map 2). The London-Glasgow line goes through Carlisle and Lancaster, at both of which you can connect with the west coast line. While the experienced cyclist will probably want to undertake the whole route in one holiday, others may wish to do only part of it. The railways give great flexibility in this respect. Unfortunately, British Rail now seems to be intent on discouraging the carriage of bikes on trains. At a time when cycling

MAP 2
THE CYCLE WAY AND THE RAILWAYS

— Cycle Way
----- Railways
--■-- Stations

TO GLASGOW AND EDINBURGH

0   10   20 KM
0   5   10   MILES

TO NEWCASTLE

BRAMPTON

CARLISLE

WIGTON

ASPATRIA

MARYPORT

LANGWATHBY

PENRITH

WORKINGTON

BRANSTY (WHITEHAVEN)

ST BEES

APPLEBY

SEASCALE

WINDERMERE

KIRKBY STEPHEN

GARSDALE HEAD

RAVENGLASS

KENDAL

MILLOM

OXEN HOLME

ULVERSTON

BARROW

GRANGE

CARNFORTH

SETTLE

LANCASTER

TO PRESTON AND THE SOUTH

TO SKIPTON AND LEEDS

N

is recovering its popularity!

As well as giving information about services and facilities, we have tried to point out things along the way that are likely to catch the cyclist's eye. These might seem insignificant, such as the type of stone in a wall, but they may lead to a closer understanding of the wider landscape. We have avoided bringing in historical or other facts about anything that cannot actually be seen from the saddle, and have ignored features near to the Cycle Way if you would have to abandon your bikes to see them.

But we have not ignored anything that you might have preferred not to have seen, like the odd chemical works or nuclear reprocessing plant! If it's there it gets a mention. And because most cyclists are observant and thoughtful folk - unlike some self-testing folks who, heads down and seeing nothing but their feet or front wheel, march or pedal off to "do" a long-distance route - we have tried to foresee their intelligent questions. "Why have a corn mill when we haven't seen any corn growing?" "Were the hills always so bare?" The Cycle Way isn't meant for endurance tests or for racing either.

Some things in this guide might clash with long-held assumptions, for example that some villages might never have had much connection with agriculture (contrary to many people's views, Cumbria has an industrial history dating from the Stone Age); or that it is often the lowest places, not the highest, that seem the least crowded. Without wishing to boast - well, not much - we know that it is not every guide that gets down to such fundamentals.

As in the official leaflet, the Cycle Way is here described in a clockwise direction (although with some attempt to cater for anti-clockwise or what we have termed widdershins riders). Going clockwise gives the benefit of following winds beside the Irish Sea, where winds from the southwest are most common. Also it gives only a gradual rise up the long Eden valley compared with a stiffer climb going anticlockwise.

We have used the seven stages described in the leaflet as a convenient basis for dividing our book. The stages link up seven towns, each described at the end of a chapter. Thus Carlisle is described at the end of Stage 7 not at the beginning of Stage 1, because we give priority to the route through the countryside. The stages are suggested in the leaflet as one-day stages for "reasonably fit persons". Although the route keeps as low as possible there are some very steep bits, such as between Barrow and Millom. People from outside Cumbria and inexperienced cyclists may well be unused to these. It's easy to overdo it. There's nothing wrong or "cheating" with using the railway, even if it's just from one station to the next. There may not, however, always be room for bikes on the trains that run along the branch-lines.

If you like maps and want something to supplement our diagrams, try Bartholomew's regular series at 1:100,000 scale. The Ordnance Survey 1:50,000 (Landranger) maps will be much more expensive because seven sheets are involved (85, 86, 89, 91, 96, 97, 98). Providing you can manage without a map for the district immediately around Barrow, only two Bartholomew's sheets are needed (nos. 34 and 38).

The Cumbria Cycle Way has been waymarked throughout (although beware of the occasional sign that has been turned in the wrong direction by some comedian). You'll develop an eye for them. However, remember that some might be on the other side of a wide main road. In the absence of a sign, keep straight on.

Finally, wherever there is no legal right of way the written permission of the landowner, and tenant if appropriate, for cyclists to follow the route has been obtained by the county council. So you shouldn't have any trouble.

Facilities

The route has the great attraction of being mostly off the tourist path. Unfortunately, this has one disadvantage: there are fewer facilities, although there is plenty of overnight accommodation in most parts. So, we have given some detail on the maps about what we feel are the essential things that the cyclist will require, particularly outside the towns and larger villages.

It is impossible to be too specific, however. Facilities change, not only from year to year but between summer and winter. For example, alterations to the licensing laws have meant that in popular tourist areas pubs are opening all day. In remoter areas, they often don't open at all at lunchtime. In some places, you can't be sure that even the public loos will be open! And unfortunately many attractions, such as museums, may be open only between Easter and September, although things are improving.

So all we've been able to do is show where it may be difficult to find something to eat and drink or somewhere to stay. For accommodation the tourist information offices are useful but they too are missing in the remote areas, though you can always phone them. Yellow pages are also valuable and free sources of information concerning some facilities; remember that bed and breakfast comes under "Guest Houses".

Our map symbols are mostly self-explanatory. The food symbol refers to public houses, hotels, cafés and restaurants, both licensed and unlicensed, where substantial meals might be obtainable. The café symbol refers to places that only serve drinks and light snacks.

KEY

BASIC FACILITIES

ABF	All Basic Facilities Including:
WC	Public Lavatory
	Public House, Hotel
	Meals
	Accommodation
	Cafe, Snack Bar
	Fish and Chip Shop, Takeaway
	Food Shop, General Shop
	Chemist
£	Bank
	Cycle Shop, Cycle Hire
	Public Telephone
PO	Post Office

ATTRACTIONS

	Museum
	Stately Home, Other Historic Building
	Garden
	Castle, Pele Tower
	Monastic Site
	Cathedral, Priory
	Monument
	Prehistoric Site
	Roman Site
	Industrial Archaeology
	Visitor Centre
	Nature Reserve

OTHER FACILITIES

	Campsite
YHA	Youth Hostel
	Tourist Information Centre
	Picnic Site
	Swimming Bath
	Railway Station

———— CCW

—·—·—· Diversions from CCW

NB Symbols indicate that at least one of that Facility is present in the area

Restaurants that only open at night and some of the larger hotels are not included. Only the well-known nature reserves are shown on the maps and mentioned in the text. We're keeping quiet about other, more vulnerable ones because publicity defeats their purpose.

Measurements

In the text, we have expressed all measurements in miles, yards, feet and inches. For those not accustomed to these units who wish to convert into metric, the following should be borne in mind. A yard is about 0.9 of a metre and there are three feet in a yard. A mile is about 1.6km so, for short distances, a reasonable approximation can be obtained by multiplying miles by one and a half.

The beginning and the end - the Caldew Bridge, Carlisle

Stage 1
Carlisle to Appleby

MAP 3
CARLISLE TO NEWBIGGIN
19 MILES (30km)
(STAGE 1)

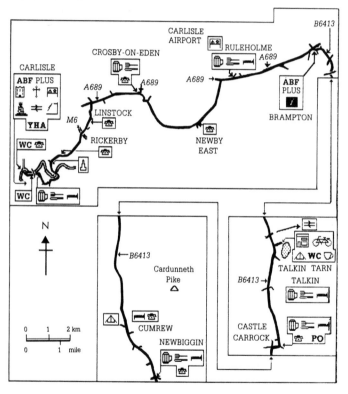

This stage takes us across the River Eden and then east to Brampton. From there it goes along the footslopes of the North Pennine escarpment, giving distant views of the Lake District fells across the broad Vale of Eden. Although almost descending to the river at Langwathby it only reaches it again at Appleby.

14

Our starting point is the bridge over the River Caldew, near to its junction with the Eden, in the public park to the north of the castle. Anyone starting from the railway station will thus go through the historic heart of the city (described briefly at the end of Stage 7) and then by subway under the busy inner ring road to the castle. A left turn after the subway and the first turning right will lead you to a car park, which you pass on your left and then bear half left down the road to the bridge. This is the very point where Hadrian's Wall crossed the Eden, to carry on westward to the Solway Firth. But you set off in the opposite direction, away from the Caldew bridge.

The Eden is below you on the left and flowing in the other direction. Remember this first view of it (if you haven't started elsewhere); your last view of the same river will be very different, in the heart of the Pennines many miles south, for it is Cumbria's greatest river. The Cycle Way skirts the park via the riverside track along an avenue of majestic trees. Where the path splits into three, take the narrow one on the left (not waymarked). This passes through a subway beneath the historic bridge that leads to Scotland. It then turns away from the river and crosses the front of the Turf Inn (the flat, riverside land below was once a race-course). A tarred alley, Zero Lane, leads to Strand Road. Go left here, between the buildings of Carlisle College of Further Education, then from the far end of this road, a path returns you to the riverside.

Memorial Bridge takes the Cycle Way across the Eden and through the well-treed Rickerby Park. Crossing flat alluvial land it passes the imposing Cumberland and Westmorland war memorial. Then through Rickerby ("Richard's settlement") along a quiet, thorn-hedged road which crosses the M6 motorway and goes through Linstock. This village is now very much a suburb of Carlisle although still retaining its pleasant green.

The Cycle Way now joins the A689 road at a point where the line of Hadrian's Wall is just to the North. But you won't be near it again until Bowness-on-Solway is reached on the final Stage. Two miles along the road, the route diverts southeastward at Crosby-on-Eden along a road signed "Little Crosby". This is well-treed and hedged country, much of it in arable farming, for between Crosby ("settlement marked with a cross") and Brampton is one of the best agricultural districts in the county. The secret is a combination, rare for Cumbria, of light freely drained soils and a sheltered climate. If you're from the Midlands, say, and trying to get away from it all, it could look a bit too much like home. Never mind: it won't last!

But there's one thing missing that is common in most other parts of England: namely, the village, with its medieval church and perhaps a green. All we have here is houses, in ones and twos, or hamlets. That's why it doesn't look complete, despite the hedges and tall trees, the arable crops and the well-fed cattle and sheep. The explanation? Of all the districts crossed by the Cycle Way, this was the most exposed to invasions from Scotland, as well as to cattle raids by neighbours, English as well as Scots.

Hobie Noble, for instance was born in Bewcastle in the North of Cumbria. But he was banished to Liddesdale across the border for his misdeeds. He didn't change his ways, however, and his execution breakfast at Carlisle is recorded in a Border ballad.

> *Then they hae tane him up thro' Carlisle town*
> *And set him by the chimney fire;*
> *They gave brave Noble a wheat loaf to eat,*
> *And that was little his desire*
>
> *They gave him a wheat loaf to eat,*
> *And after that a can o' beer. -*
> *Then they cried a' wi' ae consent,*
> *Eat brave Noble and make good cheer.*

There is no part of Cumbria where you will not find pele towers built for defence against Scottish raiders but here, on the "wrong" side of the Eden and the Irthing, was no-man's land and the land of the family feud. Settled agricultural life, leading to the growth of villages, was almost impossible at one time, though it was populous country before being transformed into war-torn waste in the first few decades of the fourteenth century. Even town life in Carlisle was badly disrupted at that time by Scottish attacks and the fires that accompanied them.

Newby East is just north of the meeting of the Irthing, coming from the uplands where Hadrian's Wall runs, and the much bigger Eden, flowing northwestward through its broad vale. When the

Planning the route - the River Eden at Carlisle
(Photo courtesy of Cumbria County Council)

The Moot Hall, Brampton

Normans conquered northern England they laid much of it waste, including the whole of northern Cumbria. Later they re-settled it with people from southern England in new villages, many of which had the suffix "by", elsewhere more commonly indicating a Danish settlement. The name, Newby, suggests a possible origin of the hamlet in this manner. Like Newton and Newbiggin (and you'll see many more of those as we go on), it is not an unusual place name in Cumbria, and they all suggest a new settlement.

A mile after Newby East, you return to the A689, a straight, wide but fairly quiet road across mainly arable land. The Irthing is crossed at Ruleholme. Civilian aircraft round here are from Carlisle airport, which houses a small but growing aviation museum, at present only open on Sunday afternoons.

And so to Brampton ("homestead or village in the brambly place"), crossing the Carlisle to Newcastle road to reach the centre of this "uncommonly attractive" little town. Thus wrote Nicolaus Pevsner in his series *The Buildings of England* (see Books Consulted), and he was never lavish in handing out praise. Most of the old buildings are a mellow red colour, being built of the local bedrock, St Bees Sandstone. There is a delightful, gently curving market street, narrowing at both ends and with yards leading to courts behind. The object was that it could be closed off quickly, with livestock brought in for safety against border raids, but this would only offer protection against minor raids. Brampton stands at the junction of four major roads and is adjacent to rich agricultural lands. Yet it failed to grow as it probably would have done in more peaceful times, because of the hindering effect of these raids. Even the development of Carlisle, protected by its castle and city walls, was hindered by them, but it hung on, to become the dominant centre of the area.

Stock up with provisions before you leave Brampton because the next shops - bar one - are at Langwathby, twenty-five miles away. You are now at the northeast corner of the Way, which next meanders generally south or southeastward along the foot of the northern Pennines. There's a sharp change to strongly rolling country and, although still with plenty of tall trees, arable cropping gives way to grass fields almost completely. You cross the railway after a couple of miles. Brampton Junction station, on the Carlisle to Newcastle upon Tyne line and some distance out of the town, can be reached by turning left shortly before the level crossing and riding east for about a mile. Only two miles from Brampton, the Talkin Tarn Country Park is worth a 300 yard diversion. Set among tall beech trees, this is the only lake near the Cycle Way. It offers a number of facilities, including the solitary shop mentioned above (see map 3).

Beyond Talkin you pass through attractive countryside with many trees, including tall roadside beeches. Stony, sandy soils lie above gravel in this rolling terrain. Towards the end of the Ice Age the steep uplands were the first to be free of ice. By contrast, the lowlands were the last, because that was where the ice sheet was thickest. So imagine the entire lowland occupied by a busily melting glacier. The flattish Pennine summits would still have local icecaps, also melting. The upland meltwater formed violent rivers, burdened with rock debris. These flooded against the margins of the lowland ice to form short-lived lakes, in which the rock and gravel were laid down. As the margin of the lowland ice shrank further away from the hills, the gravels would be gradually deposited over a wider area, in irregular heaps determined by the lie of the land and the changing conformation of the ice. The annual rainfall is just sufficient to prevent this gravelly land from being chronically droughty. (Sorry for this lengthy explanation but it may give you something to ponder over on the uphill stretches.)

The Cycle Way now crosses the River Gelt and ascends to Castle Carrock ("rock") but you won't find a castle. This is nowadays a smart commuter village near the boundary between the red sandstone of the lowlands and the grey sandstone of the Pennines. More houses are grey then red. Beyond Castle Carrock, stone walls begin to replace hedges round the fields and the countryside becomes more open. The steep slopes of the Pennine escarpment come into view on the east and will dominate the scenery for many miles. To the west the Lakeland fells become visible. It's a switchback road, broad but with surprisingly little traffic, even in summer, for such an attractive area. The trees are smaller as it is much more exposed hereabouts than at Brampton.

STAGE 1 - CARLISLE TO APPLEBY

Cumrew ("valley by the hill") has some red sandstone houses but many buildings are of grey stone from the Pennine slopes nearby. Start counting at Newbiggin ("new building or settlement"). By the time you've gone round the Cycle Way, you'll have passed six places of that name. In this village, field and barn walls are of grey sandstone while houses are of the more prestigious red. One house is a mixture of both, which is very apt for this geological boundary zone.

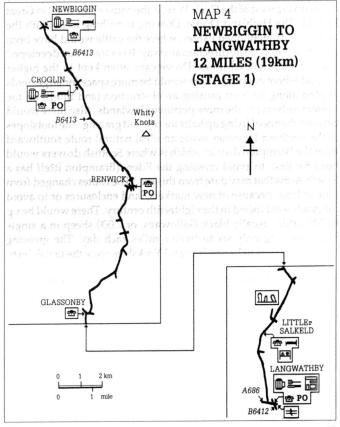

MAP 4

**NEWBIGGIN TO
LANGWATHBY
12 MILES (19km)
(STAGE 1)**

NEWBIGGIN

B6413

CROGLIN

PO

B6413

Whity
Knots

N

RENWICK

PO

GLASSONBY

LITTLE-
SALKELD

LANGWATHBY

A686

PO

B6412

0   1   2 km

0   1   mile

There's a great feeling of space, partly because it is high up, partly because this is a drove road, with wide green verges, and partly because of the stone walls which are lower than most thorn hedges. (They also give less protection from the wind. You might wish for less scenery and more shelter.) Another feature of drove ways is the hollow-way or sunken road; and just before Croglin our road runs between sloping banks where generations of Scottish cattle have worn a gully through a bit of softer ground on their way to English markets. A legacy they also seem to have left, only a mile or two to the west of the Cycle Way, is the name of the hotel in Great Salkeld, The Highland Drove. Droving is nothing to do with the Border raids mentioned earlier, where the cattle would have been driven in the opposite direction anyway! It is a trade that developed later, in more settled times. Droveways often kept to the higher ground where possible. There would be more space for large herds to plod along without causing an obstruction (and mud!) on the busier roadways in the more populous lowlands. Also there would be more chance of fixing up halts for rest and grazing. The footslopes of the northern Pennines made an ideal natural route southward from the Brampton district which is where Scottish drovers would head for first, to avoid crossing the Eden. (Brampton itself has a Scotch Arms that may date from this era.) The routes changed from time to time, because of new markets, land enclosures or to avoid toll roads established in the eighteenth century. There would be up to 200 cattle, usually black Galloways, or 2,000 sheep in a single herd, covering only six to twelve miles each day. The growing industrial towns of Lancashire and Yorkshire were the usual destinations.

Croglin ("bend in the torrent") is yet another of the many villages that characterise this district, small but at least contributing to a more English-looking countryside than between Carlisle and Brampton, although it was lusher there. It was just, but only just, not quite so exposed to the Scottish border raids. This village, like many more to come, is built entirely of red sandstone, which is the bedrock for many miles onward. Oh - and there's one more thing about Croglin - if you meet a creature with "a hideous brown face with flaming eyes", according to Augustus Hare, the writer, ignore it. It's just the local vampire, thinking about lunch. Most cyclists get through all right, although the prudent might wish to keep their necks covered. Seriously though, the legend of the Croglin Vampire is reputed to have inspired Bram Stoker, who lived over on the east coast at Whitby, to invent Dracula.

Assuming that you have come through Croglin intact, you carry on for a short time further on the B6413 but, where it swings west in the direction of Lazonby and the fleshpots of Penrith, you continue to press on resolutely in a southeasterly direction for a short while. This was still a drove way, to judge by its widely spaced walls; but you leave it after Renwick ("Hrafn's village or dairy farm"), where the Way starts descending towards the Eden valley. The hummocky gravel terrain has now given way to smoother ground, reflecting the lie of the red sandstone bedrock which is not far below the sandy soil. Near the turn-off southwestward to Glassonby, however, ditches alongside the road and rushes in the fields suggest a patch of glacial drift (boulder clay), which becomes predominant further up the Eden valley. Straight-sided rectangular fields, probably drawn on plans in a solicitor's office, suggest that this land was among the last to be enclosed, in the late eighteenth or early nineteenth centuries.

The descent steepens and there are magnificent views towards the Lake District fells, with Saddleback showing why it is so named. At Glassonby ("Glassan's settlement") we have reached more sheltered countryside. After a right turn at a crossroads just past the village, there is an elegant mansion on the right. Straight after that and also on the right, is a gateway through which a single standing stone can be seen. This monolith is associated with a stone circle, the biggest in Cumbria, known as Long Meg and Her Daughters. About half a mile from the Cycle Way, a visit is well worth the short diversion. The site is dotted with mature ash trees, which indicates more lime in the soil than normal in this sandstone district. (A surfeit of bones, perhaps?) Long Meg lies outside the circle and it is said that a line from the centre of the circle, through her, points to where the sun sets in midwinter. It is tempting to think that they built the circle so that they would know when to get out the booze to celebrate the imminent return of the sun (after all, we still do it), but surely they could have done it without going to all that trouble.

Another theory holds that people were turned into stone for

dancing on Sunday but in 1698 that intrepid traveller, Celia Fiennes, wrote of "Great Mag" that those "soliciting her to an unlawfull love by an enchantment are turned with her into stone". This resembles the story of the Propoetides, girls of Cyprus who foolishly denied the divinity of Aphrodite, the goddess of love. To punish them, she first "inspired in them such immodesty that, losing all sense of shame, they would prostitute themselves to all comers. In the end they were turned into rocks" (*Larousse Encyclopedia of Mythology*).

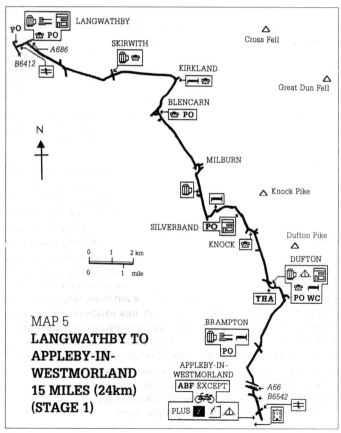

MAP 5
**LANGWATHBY TO
APPLEBY-IN-
WESTMORLAND
15 MILES (24km)
(STAGE 1)**

As there are no such stone circles in Cyprus, can these be they? (But surely there were never goings-on like that in Cumbria.)

Taking care not to annoy the gods, you press on down to Little Salkeld ("spring by willows"). It has an elegant eighteenth-century hall built almost beside the River Eden, which you haven't been near for many miles. You follow the river upstream, between hedges again and with more traffic on the road, to Langwathby ("settlement by the long ford"). The largest village since Brampton, this is a local centre, with a large mill that produces animal food-stuffs, a major employer in this rural area. It also has a railway station, the first since Brampton and also the first you have come across on the Settle-Carlisle line - but by no means the last.

Stock up again before you leave Langwathby, because there aren't many shops between here and Appleby, or places where you can get meals. Villages round here whose population was originally completely dependent upon the land around them are not like that now. As in so many other areas of England, only a small number of the working population is still in farming. For generations now, young people have been able to obtain easier work than that on the land, with shorter hours and more pay, mostly in towns. In response, agriculture has adopted labour-saving practices. As a result, most of the working population daily travels long distances to their places of work. Some were born in the village and have chosen to commute rather than move away. Others are people from else-where who have deliberately chosen to live in a village, at the expense of a long daily drive to work. Others still are retired. This means that the social make-up of most villages is much the same as that of any town or suburb. And it means that people shop in urban supermarkets or out-of-town shopping centres, so the village shops have to close down or become highly specialised (antiques for instance). This is a pity because they used to be social centres where people went as much for a chat as to buy provisions.

But, dashing a nostalgic tear from the eye, we must get on! Heading back towards the Pennine escarpment from Langwathby, the Cycle Way follows the Alston road (A686) for a quarter of a mile before turning off for Skirwith ("woodland used by men of the district"). The land has a markedly even configuration, for again the sandstone rock is near the surface with only a sandy soil above it.

Because it was infertile it was not enclosed until late, as the dead-straight road and the rectangular field boundaries prove. This was possibly done at the time of the Napoleonic Wars, when more land came under the plough than has done ever since, even during the two World Wars. The Ordnance Survey 1:50,000 map calls it Langwathby Moor but most of it is farmed now. Indeed, the lightness of the land makes cultivation possible without damaging the soil, a rare chance in the Cumbrian climate. You'll see cereals, potatoes and turnips here. Artificial fertilizers make up for the natural infertility, which is shown by a few patches of acid-tolerant birch and oak scrub. Tree growth improves just before Skirwith where tall beeches and oaks line the road and embellish a private park. The village is scattered on a green with a rushing stream in the middle.

There is now a gradual climb along a wide roadway across more open, stone-walled country towards Kirkland ("land belonging to church") with a superb view towards Cross Fell (2,930 feet) and the Dun Fells. The glistening dome on Great Dun Fell is a radio installation for the guidance of civil aircraft on the air lane to North America (marked in clear weather by the large number of vapour trails). If you have a map it might show "Hanging Walls of Mark Anthony". These are medieval cultivation terraces, half a mile from Kirkland and the Cycle Way but there are some visible from the road near Nateby (Stage 2). Having climbed to Kirkland, the Way simply turns round and goes down again. Don't blame us. At least you get some excellent views of the Lake District fells. The next village, Blencarn ("hilltop and rock pile"), has a mixture of building stone, the older buildings being of red sandstone. There is a rectangular green here - and you'll be seeing more. If, by chance, you happen to be carrying a rod and line you can fish for rainbow trout in the artificial lake at the approach to the village.

The country is more hummocky hereabouts and thorn hedges are common, because you are crossing a mantle of fairly heavy boulder clay left at the end of the Ice Age. This often takes the form of oval-shaped ridges, some of which are as much as a mile long, known as "drumlins". Their "egg-basket topography" will be seen in many places along the Way. Geologists disagree as to how the drift was formed into these repeated shapes. Because it has been dragged along beneath the ice from many different sources, the drift is less infertile than the shallow sandstone soils at Langwathby, which is why there are several tall ash trees in the hedges. They don't like poor soils.

The narrow road now leads into what used to be Westmorland (so far, you've been in the former county of Cumberland), starting with a flourish in the magnificent village of Milburn ("mill stream"). This is a much-quoted example of a sort of inward-facing village around a rectangular green found on both sides of the Pennines. Built in medieval times for protection against Scottish raids, the villages had narrow entrances at the corners that were walled-up every winter (the raiding season usually only began after the crops were in), leaving only narrow, easily-defensible gaps between the houses. Livestock would be driven on to the large green when raiders approached. South of Milburn there's a sign leading to Newbiggin nearby while there's another some miles beyond Penrith, the only one not close to the Way. (Are you keeping count?)

Just past the pub at Gullom Holme, somebody has been practising topiary in the roadside hedge. Beyond this, the Way turns off, past Slakes Farm to Silverband, where there is a shop at the garage. (There is a Silverband Mine on the high slopes of Great Dun Fell still producing barytes.) From here, good views can be had of steep conical hills at the edge of the Pennine escarpment, each of which is called a Pike and takes it name from the nearest village. The nearest one to the Cycle Way is Knock Pike. These are not made of either of the two sorts of bedrock that we've been seeing all along the escarpment (Eden valley red sandstone and the grey sandstone of the Pennines), but consist of older, mostly volcanic rock, which has been brought to the surface by faults and thrusts. Where the bedrock is surrounded by newer rocks in this way, it is called an "inlier". This example is famous to geologists and is called the Cross Fell Inlier. It certainly enhances the scenery along this part of the escarpment.

From Knock ("hillock") a narrow road leads to Dufton ("farmstead where doves were kept") which gives its name to the next pike. This is another attractive "green" village (nothing to do with its politics), with more facilities than any other village along the escarpment, unfortunately not including pub food. You're back on the red standstone here, as the buildings show. Some are colour-washed with the window-lintels painted in a darker shade, in the traditional Cumbrian (and Scottish) way. Dufton Hall is worth a glimpse through its imposing gateway on the village green. It's the first one of two interesting buildings on the Cycle Way that were mysteriously overlooked by Pevsner (see Books Consulted). You can't miss it - it's opposite to the public lavatory! (Now *that* deserves a mention. It's the best on the Cycle Way.)

Incidentally, don't be surprised here if you see earnest-looking people, bearing heavy rucksacks. Dufton is on another strenuous route, the Pennine Way, and walkers have a right to look earnest because they still have a long, arduous way to go before downing the half pint that Wainwright promised all those who finish it. (Er, no! We're not doing the same.) If you stay overnight, you should be able to exchange moans with these adventurous souls.

As well as its geological phenomenon, the Cross Fell escarpment has a climatic one too, the Helm Wind. When a strong, northeast wind blows off the Cross Fell plateau, to quote from the Meteorological Glossary, "... a slender, nearly stationary roll of whirling cloud (the Helm Bar) appears in mid-air..." The cold wind blows strongly down the steep fell sides until it comes nearly under the Bar, when it suddenly ceases. Approaching this point it is characteristically very gusty and may cause structural damage. It retards grass growth and is a menace at lambing time. J.Oliver Wilson wrote, "Frequently, when there is not even a gentle breeze in the valley, the Helm may be heard miles away on the fells roaring like the sea." One of us has experienced this wind, waking at Dufton one morning to hear a roaring, although the leaves of the sycamore outside his window were not moving. After breakfast he drove up the road to Keisley, the highest village in the district. The wind was at ground level here and almost wrenched the car door off when he opened it. It was not a day for cycling. No wonder the buildings are all so solid along the escarpment.

Beyond Dufton you push off down into more sheltered country, the Cycle Way rising and falling steeply as it crosses more drumlins. Brampton (another one - but smaller!), although slightly off the route, gives an opportunity for those who vainly sought food in Dufton to catch up with a bar snack. After Brampton comes a final

The Moot Hall and Church, Appleby

descent, with a view of Appleby Castle, to an underpass under the busy Scotch Corner to Penrith road. Then into the red-sandstone market town itself, by a right turn on to a bridge over the River Eden, more than forty miles from where you last crossed it on the outskirts of Carlisle.

The original Appleby ("farmstead with an apple tree") was on the east side of the river, opposite the castle, where the original parish church still stands. The present town centre across the bridge was deliberately planned in the twelfth century. It didn't just grow, like Brampton and indeed most market towns. Boroughgate, the wide main street bordered by lime trees, running up from the porticoed gate of St Lawrence's Church to the castle, is the finest street along the Cycle Way, if not in Cumbria. There are some handsome Georgian houses on the west side and some attractive old almshouses on the east, with the late sixteenth-century Moot Hall, home of the Tourist Information Office, in the middle of the road at the bottom. John Wesley, the much-travelled evangelist, came here in 1766 and wrote in his Journal, with surprising sarcasm: "a county town worthy of Ireland, containing at least five and twenty houses". Perhaps he had been travelling too much.

The Castle, once owned by that redoubtable castle-owner Lady Anne Clifford (of whom more later), has a long history and is well worth a visit. It is also the centre of the Rare Breeds Survival Trust, with a half-mile nature trail. The presence of the Castle, however, did not always save the town from the depredations of the Scots and it had its share of being burnt to the ground.

Appleby was originally the county town of northern Westmorland, before the Barony of Appleby was merged with that of Kirkby-in-Kentdale (ie. Kendal) to form the county of Westmorland. (Its present official name of Appleby-in-Westmorland was only adopted as a sentimental gesture after Westmorland was amalgamated with Cumberland in 1974 to form the county of Cumbria.) It was an important market for cattle brought by the

Main Street, Appleby, from the Castle gates

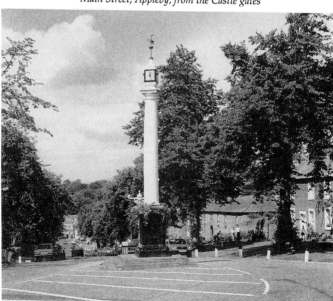

Scottish drovers. Until recently it was still an important market town, despite the competing attractions of Penrith. However, it has now lost most of its traditional market-town industries, including the brewery which is now just a brewer's depot (and not a local brewer either). Nowadays many of the men, and the single women, commute to work in Penrith, or even Carlisle. On the other hand others, women particularly, come in from the rural areas to work in the town. One traditional rural industry has survived in the form of Express Dairy's milk-processing plant at the edge of Appleby, which provides well-needed jobs. Appleby also has a growing tourist industry, boosted by the Horse Fair at the end of June, when travelling people come from far and wide. This is followed by the Appleby Festival during the first two weeks of July. The proposed closure, now avoided, of the Settle-Carlisle line would have involved closing the town's railway station. That would have been a blow to the tourist industry as well as to people commuting to Carlisle.

Enclosure road south of Appleby

Stage 2
Appleby to Kirkby Lonsdale

This quiet stage falls into three sections: (1) the Vale of Eden drumlin country, which the Cycle Way entered shortly before Appleby; (2) the Pennine dales of Mallerstang, which you go up, not too steeply, and Garsdale, down which you freewheel to Sedbergh and; (3) The Lune valley. Each section finishes at a market town - Kirkby Stephen, Sedbergh and Kirkby Lonsdale - but villages are rare.

From Appleby Castle the first mile is along the road to Tebay and Kendal (B6260), which became a toll road as early as 1760, an indication that Appleby and Kendal were then the two principal towns in Westmorland. It goes past a well-managed farm called Slosh. This means "watery mud" (*Collins Concise Dictionary*), which is what all this district would quickly become in winter if over-stocked with cattle. Perhaps somebody once did that here. As you'll see all around, the soil makes first-class permanent grassland. This is fortunate because it is rarely dry enough to be cultivated by heavy modern machinery without becoming a sticky mess.

The Cycle Way then turns off down the Soulby road across rolling, well-hedged drumlin country. When the land was first cleared and farmed there were insufficient stones to be cleared from the soil and disposed of by using them for field walls, hence the hedges. Rushes, willows and drainage ditches at the roadside are a reminder of what this land would look like if it were not artificially drained. This may be why there are no villages here, after the succession of them in Stage 1, as we got further from the Scottish border. Before modern times, villages had to be self-sufficient to a large extent. They had to grow their own corn, for example, so they couldn't devote all their land to the one crop that most of Cumbria is so well suited to, grass. They shunned water-retentive clay soils that were difficult to cultivate. Consequently such land was among the last to be enclosed, usually in the late eighteenth or early nineteenth century. As we have seen, enclosures of that period are straight-edged, rectangular fields, with isolated farmsteads. The farming population was thus scattered, rather than concentrated in villages, and the new holdings were served by roads of drawing-board straightness regardless of the lie of the land. The Cycle Way follows one of these across the rolling countryside. Its straightness is compensated for by the roadside flowers. Cowslips abound in mid-May, giving way to a profusion of species in midsummer, making this possibly the most colourful stretch of the Cycle Way.

Wind-bent trees mark the highest point of this section, after which you start the descent to Soulby. Wild Boar Fell stands up to the south, like Table Mountain. There are also good views northeastward to the Pennine escarpment. You might hear gunfire from a military range over there. Soulby has an attractive green, crossed by a stream and containing a stone-built pound for stray animals (to the right as you cross the bridge). This is still drumlin

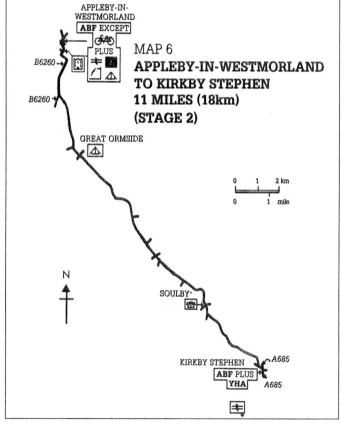

Langwathby (Photo courtesy of Cumbria County Council)
Dufton

The Moorcock Inn, Garsdale Head
The Howgill Fells, from the Sedgwick Geological Trail panel

*Kirkby Stephen market place, with porticoed entrance to
the church on the left*

country but signs of a change come soon: stone walls reappear for
the first time since you moved away from the Cross Fell escarpment
near Dufton in Stage 1. The stone now is a light grey limestone,
which becomes very evident as you enter Kirkby Stephen ("church
town by the Eden"; it is purely coincidence that the parish church
is dedicated to St Stephen).

As at Dufton, the Cycle Way here intersects a long-distance
walk, signified by the presence of the "Coast-to-Coast Chip Shop".
(Will we shortly see a discreet "Cumbria Cycle Way Oysters and
Champagne Bar"?) There's no shortage of bed and breakfast
accommodation, but note that much of it is along the Tebay road,
past the turn-off on to the Nateby road that is followed by the Cycle
Way. This pleasant market town was once, like Appleby, a market
for Scottish cattle. It is still very much an agricultural centre, but it
also used to be an important woollen knitting centre and at one time
had a cotton mill too. It lay close to the way across the Pennines by

33

Stainmore that has been followed since prehistoric times. Even now, during the Blackpool illuminations in the autumn, the town is full of coaches from the northeast going to or returning from "the lights". It grew considerably during the Railway Age, being at the junction of two railways. The Settle-Carlisle line still functions, thanks to the efforts of many who were determined that it wouldn't close, but the Darlington to Tebay and Penrith line across Stainmore was closed during the Beeching era.

St Stephen's Church, its red sandstone contrasting with most other buildings, looks handsome from the Market Place, viewed across the grass from an early nineteenth-century portico at the churchyard gate, a feature the town shares with Appleby. Look closely at the stones of the older houses. They are of brockram, known to geologists as a breccia (a rock composed of angular fragments cemented naturally together) and in this case the fragments are of limestone. Another feature in Kirkby Stephen - unique along the Cycle Way and rare enough anywhere in Cumbria - is the building containing Barclays Bank. If you can manage not to arouse the suspicions of the police (they may think your bike is a new twist to the getaway car), take a good look at it from across the street. It is a delightful example of the quaint, whimsical, asymmetric Art Nouveau style of architecture popular in Edwardian times. Just look at those chimneys!

The Cycle Way now leaves the A685 (which goes on to Newbiggin-on-Lune a few miles further west, so that's another to add to the list) and follows the Nateby road (B6259) past a grandiose mid-Victorian Temperance Institute, its weathered red sandstone the last to be seen for a long way. You are quickly back in the country, with limestone field-walls everywhere and the lime-loving ash the commonest tree. Just before Nateby the road crosses the River Eden. At the same time it passes over the track of the old railway line that went across Stainmore to Barnard Castle and Darlington. This was built to carry coal from the Durham coalfields to the iron and steel industry of West Cumbria (of which more later). Nateby itself sports a 1920s Automobile Association yellow place-name disc, which states "London 266 1/4". There's precision for you! There's only one other on the Cycle Way, plus another within a short distance of it. Most were removed during the 1940 invasion scare.

This was in the strange belief that, with neither these nor signposts, the Germans couldn't possibly know where they were. The sign is on the wall of the pub, the Black Bull, which together with the Black Bull Hotel in Kirkby Stephen, was named in cattle-droving times. Black cattle were nearly always from Scotland.

The landscape starts to close in as we enter Mallerstang, the name given to the upper valley of the Eden, a sprightlier stream than in Carlisle where you first saw it. The climate is harsher here, with

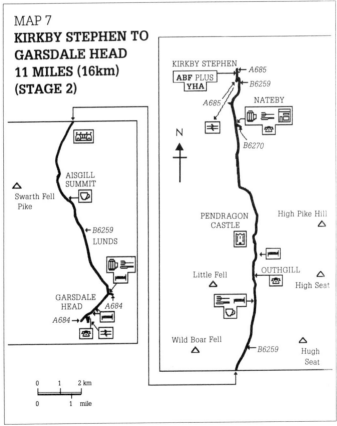

MAP 7
KIRKBY STEPHEN TO GARSDALE HEAD
11 MILES (16km)
(STAGE 2)

KIRKBY STEPHEN — A685
ABF PLUS — B6259
YHA
A685
NATEBY
B6270

AISGILL
SUMMIT

△
Swarth Fell
Pike

PENDRAGON
CASTLE

High Pike Hill
△

←B6259
LUNDS

Little Fell
△

OUTHGILL
High Seat
△

GARSDALE
HEAD A684
A684→

Wild Boar Fell
△

←B6259 Hugh
Seat
△

N
↑

0 1 2 km
0 1 mile

more rainfall and a shorter growing season: trees are smaller and rushes are more of a problem on farmland. The original road was on the west side of the river and still exists as a track, going past Wharton Hall (the Whartons were the local aristocracy in medieval times). The remains of Hartley Castle, just to the east of Kirkby Stephen, and Pendragon Castle show the importance of Mallerstang as a route. There are prehistoric remains as well. Later a drove road, then a toll road (Kirkby Stephen-Hawes) as late as 1825, the original road finally became part of the route of the Settle-Carlisle railway line. Here, the line is also west of the river and less visible than higher up the dale.

One mile south of Nateby, two fields north of White Brackens Farm but on the east side of the road, there is a set of medieval cultivation terraces across the hillside. They are more easily seen by widdershins riders. These were the result of the open-field system which began to be replaced about 1600 by the hedged enclosures that we see today. (Human nature being what it is, there were as many objections to these enclosures as there are today when hedges are being pulled up again.) Previously the cultivable land was shared out in the form of long narrow strips. Each villager had a handful of these, scattered all over the parish. They preferred long narrow strips because they used oxen for ploughing; and the fewer times ox-teams have to be manoeuvred round at the end of a furrow, the better. When these parallel strips, or "reans" as they were called, were laid out across a slope, the act of ploughing year after year resulted in soil being moved from the inner side to the outer, with each rean finishing up as a kind of terrace.

Pendragon Castle stands at the roadside near a bridge over the river. It was built in the twelfth century by Hugh de Morville, one of the four who, in 1170, murdered St Thomas à Becket, the Archbishop of Canterbury. The Scots burnt it in 1541, but it was restored in 1660 by Lady Anne Clifford, a great restorer of castles, including Brougham near Penrith, Appleby, Brough and Skipton. The latter was in the then West Riding of Yorkshire many miles to the south, so she must have been a great traveller as well. The name, Pendragon, has a suspiciously "antiquarian" air, redolent of the Arthurian legend, and is unlikely to be the original one. Legend maintains, however, that Uther Pendragon, Arthur's father, built it

Pendragon Castle

and that he unsuccessfully tried to divert the Eden to form a moat.
Hence the rhyme:

> *Let Uther Pendragon do what he can,*
> *Eden will run where Eden ran.*

It is good to hear that the present owner is emulating Lady Anne
and has repaired and restored the ruin.

Just south of the Thrang Hotel a quiet lane leads down to the
river, which it crosses via Thrang Bridge (this is the line of the old
road). The name "thrang" (throng) is the only reminder that this
was once a meeting place, of packhorse men trading a great variety
of merchandise. Mallerstang links at its head with both Wensleydale
and Garsdale, making a relatively low, three-way passage through
the Pennines. Traders came from all three directions to exchange
goods here. Those from Wensleydale would use the old drove road,
higher but shorter, leaving the present road on the left after the
Thrang lane. Ings Mead, a mile south, is now a falconry centre, open
to the public in the summer months.

Wild Boar Fell is not to be confused with its southern neighbour

Hellgill Force

- Great Baugh Fell - which you will be seeing before long. Impressive to the southwest, its table-mountain outline has been replaced by a more pointed shape. The western side of the valley has a stepped appearance caused by a succession of sandstone and limestone crags. These rock layers alternate with soft shales, which give rise to less steep, hummocky, rush-covered ground. There is a stepped series of waterfalls near Elm Gill. The infant Eden plummets over a handsome one which can be seen in the distance from Aisgill Farm. To the east, the cliffs of Mallerstang Edge stand out. One of these eastern fells, Hugh Seat, is named after the previously-mentioned Hugh de Morville. To the east of Outhgill, the only village in the dale, seams of coal were worked for local domestic use and to burn limestone.

The road gradually climbs to the level of the Settle-Carlisle railway and then to the watershed, the highest point of the Cycle Way at 1,194 feet. It then enters the very beginning of Wensleydale. Instead of running towards the Solway Firth and thence the Irish Sea, the water in the streams here ends up in the North Sea via the Humber estuary. Just beyond the summit a lane is signposted to Hellgill, quarter of a mile along which is Hellgill Force, the nearest waterfall to the Cycle Way and well worth a look. (You can take your bike.) This is the last you'll see of the Eden until you're back in Carlisle.

Except for salt marshes at the coast, this is the "wildest" looking stretch of country along the Cycle Way but, remember, it is all part of a farming system. Every bit of the hill land is grazed, even if only by a handful of sheep. The vegetation, rough though it may be, is converted by them into wool and mutton. Trees survive only where sheep cannot reach. So the hills are bare except for the odd tree clinging to the side of a ravine. Climate has nothing to do with it. Without sheep, trees would eventually grow everywhere you can see. "Wild nature" hereabouts would mean forest, not moorland.

The Cycle Way slips into Yorkshire for three miles and simultaneously, but for much longer, into the Yorkshire Dales National Park. Puzzled? So are the locals (see below). After going under the railway, the road gives a view over the scattered township of Lunds, with some small but well-shaped drumlins next to the road. Be sure to turn west (right) on reaching the A684 road at the Moorcock Inn, or the Tykes will get you and convert you into a Yorkshire pudding or, more likely round here, a Wensleydale cheese. Apart from this junction it's difficult to get lost between

Nateby and Sedbergh. Incidentally, this is the easternmost point of the Cycle Way. A half-mile climb takes you back under the railway, into Cumbria and over another watershed, from which the water flows into the Lune and finally into the Irish Sea near Lancaster. There is a railway station at Garsdale Head, your last chance to opt out for many a mile, after which the Settle-Carlisle line vanishes to the south.

Unless you are a widdershins rider, and these too will get their reward before long on the descent through Mallerstang, it's now downhill almost all the way through Garsdale ("Garth's valley") with lovely views of the river Clough, tumbling past crags and woods. For several miles the road is bound on the right by the long southern flank of Great Baugh Fell and on the left by the ridge between Snaizwold Fell and Aye Gill Pike.

The Yorkshire Dales National Park, through which you are now passing, was set up before the reorganisation of counties in 1974.

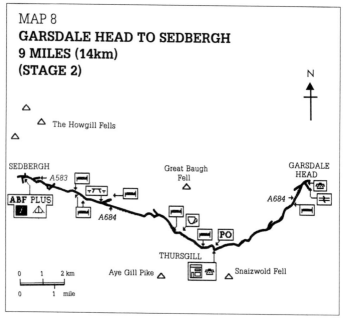

MAP 8
GARSDALE HEAD TO SEDBERGH
9 MILES (14km)
(STAGE 2)

N

The Howgill Fells

SEDBERGH
A583

Great Baugh
Fell

GARSDALE
HEAD

A684

ABF PLUS

A684

THURSGILL

Aye Gill Pike

Snaizwold Fell

0   1   2 km

0   1   mile

The Howgills from Lower Garsdale

The part round Sedbergh used to be in the West Riding of Yorkshire but then found itself in the new county of Cumbria. However, it stayed in the YDNP, the rest of which is now all in North Yorkshire.

Garsdale has more trees and is less gaunt than Mallerstang, although the geology is the same. In the upper parts there's a repetition of sandstones, limestones and shales; lower in the valley there is solid limestone. From where you cross the river for the second time, the Howgill Fells start dominating the view ahead. Before long the road enters unfenced land from which there is a really fine view of them, with their bracken-covered midriff and the Sedbergh lowland in front. The Sedgwick Geological Trail is explained in a panel in the big lay-by here. This commemorates the bicentenary of the birth of a famous geologist, Adam Sedgwick, at Dent in the valley to the south. The road follows the river for about one mile and crosses the Dent Fault, first described and interpreted by Sedgwick. This fault marks the edge of the Pennine rocks. The

41

repeated sequence of different rock layers, roughly horizontal, gives way here to a solid mass of dark grey slates and fine-grained sandstones.

Cross the river once again, now swollen by the waters of the Rawthey from the northeast, and enter the small town of Sedbergh. Another long-distance footpath, the Dales Way, which runs from Ilkley to Windermere, intersects here, so there's a chance of meeting other adventurers, as at Dufton and Kirkby Stephen. Sedbergh has the most dramatic setting of all the market towns on our route, with Winder, the southernmost bastion of the Howgill Fells, rising steeply behind it.

The parish church is long and low. The cyclist-unfriendly cobbled main street is luckily followed only by those going anticlockwise (a good enough reason for travelling clockwise). There's a famous

Cyclists forced to dismount, Sedbergh

public school which provides by far the largest share of local employment, most other workers having to go daily to Kendal. Like Kirkby Stephen, the town used to have both a woollen and a cotton industry but these declined many years ago. As early as the beginning of the nineteenth century an express coach route from Kendal to Newcastle used the toll road to Kirkby Stephen up the Rawthey valley. The town was also on the Kendal to Askrigg toll road, the one you have just descended but, fortunately these days, without having

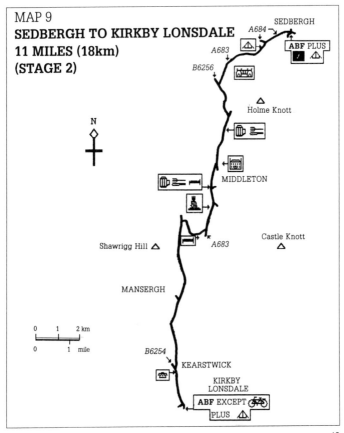

MAP 9
SEDBERGH TO KIRKBY LONSDALE
11 MILES (18km)
(STAGE 2)

to pay anything. This is the road that connected with the Kirkby Stephen-Hawes toll at the Moorcock Inn. However, Sedbergh was an important route centre long before the toll roads, as is shown by the remains of an old Norman motte and bailey castle above the town. It also used to be on the old London and North Western railway line from Kirkby Stephen to Tebay, the route of which you will be near for part of the way towards Kirkby Lonsdale.

At Briggflatts, one and a quarter miles from Sedbergh, is a famous Friends' Meeting House, dated 1675, the oldest in the north of England, unspoilt and with mullioned windows. The Sedbergh area has close connections with Quakerism whose founder George Fox often held meetings hereabouts. The Cycle Way crosses the Rawthey for the last time, just before its confluence with the Lune, which shortly appears beside the road, as you enter prosperous-looking countryside, with woods and tall hedgerow trees. This is lowland English scenery at its best although still surrounded by hills. Half a mile after the Lune bridge, a sign points to Holme Farm, a mile along a side road. This is an "open farm", with conducted tours, seasonal demonstrations, local sheep breeds, a protected badger sett and other attractions.

The disused railway track is still much in evidence and you are also running near the line of the old Roman road that ran from

*The Roman milestone
at Middleton*

Legion headquarters at Chester to Carlisle on the Wall. The Legion was quartered at Chester, with the Wall being manned by auxiliary troops, but in an emergency it could be marched along this road through the Lune valley in double-quick time. After the enclosed nature of Mallerstang and Garsdale, the Lune valley appears open and becomes even more so as you progress south. Just before Middleton, the fifteenth century Middleton Hall is on the left, shielded from view by a medieval wall with an archway. There is public access to it through a bustling, dog-barking farmyard. The existence of a house of this period shows that this area was less devastated by the Scots than the land further north. Significantly, just after the Swan at Middleton, the road now lurches to the left whereas the Roman road went straight on uncompromisingly. A Roman milestone has been re-erected in a field near Middleton Church on the old road line. Maybe this is where G.K.Chesterton wrote:

> *Before the Roman came to Rye or out to Severn strode,*
> *The rolling English drunkard made the rolling English road.*

About a mile further south, the route turns off the A683 and crosses the river by an iron bridge. The west side of the valley is dominated by Rigmaden Hall. The road, with iron-rail fences, winds uphill to the parkland surrounding the mansion, though from here you can only see the hall by looking back over your shoulder after you have passed it. Widdershins riders get a much better view. From this very quiet road there are fine views over the valley to the Barbon fells and, after the Mansergh turning, down to the river. Arrival at the B6254 at Kearstwick ("valley clearing") signals the end of this pastoral stretch and the beginning of the town of Kirkby Lonsdale ("the settlement with a church in the Lune valley" - to distinguish it from Kirkby Kentdale, now known simply as Kendal, in the next valley to the west).

The perfection of the landscape in this stretch of the Lune valley captivated John Ruskin, the Victorian author and art critic, who wrote that it was "one of the loveliest scenes in England". Follow the signs past the churchyard to "Ruskin's View", later painted by Turner. Kirkby Lonsdale is another of the splendid market towns the route has passed through since Brampton, with many attractive buildings from different periods along the narrow streets. St Mary's is the best Norman church in Cumbria and the finest town church on the Cycle Way. In the valley bottom to the south of the town the famous three-arched Devil's Bridge spans the Lune where it flows through a cleft in the limestone. For you are into limestone country from now on and for a much longer stretch than on the first occasion, south of Kirkby Stephen.

Market Place, Kirkby Lonsdale

The tide coming in at Arnside

Stage 3
Kirkby Lonsdale to Ulverston

Things are different when you leave Kirkby Lonsdale. For one thing, the route veers westward away from the Lune valley and heads for the coast at Arnside. For another, the bedrock is now limestone. This light grey stone has been used in buildings and dry-stone walls, which contrast with green grass fields to make a mellow and distinctive landscape. From here to Arnside, the Lancashire Cycle Way follows the same route as its Cumbria counterpart, although it is only waymarked near Arnside.

The pleasant group of old buildings at High Biggins includes the original Elizabethan or Stuart Biggins Hall. With its mullioned windows blocked up, it's now used as a barn. The present house was built in 1895. High hedges block the view somewhat in this land of well-drained loamy soils overlying limestone. One mile beyond High Biggins, through a gate on the north side of the road beside a sign announcing "Bridleway to Hollin Hall and Sealford", is a roughly oval Romano-British enclosure bounded by a low embankment with some stones upstanding. Go through two gates set close together and look half left. An ash tree stands in the centre. The rocky areas round it are natural exposures of the limestone bedrock.

Hutton Roof ("farmstead near the end of a hill" - Roof a personal name, Rufus originally?) is a quiet little village overshadowed by impressive limestone crags. Once famous for building stone, long-abandoned quarried land is visible through gaps in the hedge on the left just before the village. (There's another village of the same name a few miles north of Penrith.) If you turn left instead of right on entering the village, you will find a little way down the road the village name proclaimed upon a yellow metal AA disc, similar to the one at Nateby and just as precise: "London 252$^{1}/_{4}$". On returning to the Cycle Way proper, there's a post office on the left offering "drinks, sweets and crisps" as well as a telephone box. Make the most of these facilities, it will be Arnside before you find another shop.

The Cycle Way goes via a deep, narrow lane, between tall hedges and with a grass strip in the middle, to another Newbiggin. The quiet lane is then more open, looking like an old drovers' way, and eventually runs unfenced through bracken and gorse at the foot of Farleton Fell. Then it plunges between honeysuckle-festooned hedges again as a sunken lane reminiscent of Devon. These lanes between High Biggins and Farleton are the most hedged-in sections of the entire route.

Farleton Fell ("the fell by Faerela's farmstead") stands impressively to the east of the village of that name. There are no facilities here, even the phone box marked on the Ordnance Survey map has disappeared. To the west is a trough-like depression from which, if the wind is in the right quarter, you may hear the Niagara-

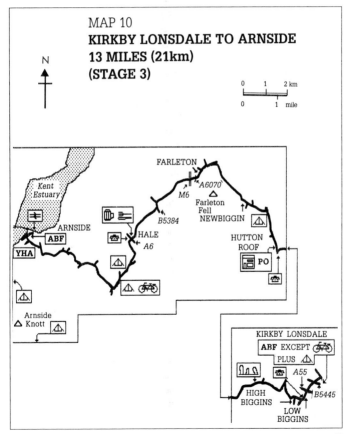

MAP 10
KIRKBY LONSDALE TO ARNSIDE
13 MILES (21km)
(STAGE 3)

like roar of motorway traffic. All the great routes to Scotland via the west side of England are bunched together here: the old coach road, now the A6070, the M6 motorway, the London-Glasgow railway, and the A6 trunk road. North Sea gas ducts run underground, electricity above, and there are also remnants of the Lancaster-Kendal canal. This you cross via the elegant Duke's Bridge, just beyond the A6070. Severed by the motorway and thus ruined, this ex-waterway is now cynically signposted on the M6 as a tourist attraction! Between here and the A6, a mild and sheltered climate, together with mostly well-drained undulating land, make cereal-growing worth the effort - the first you've seen since Langwathby. Another thing you haven't yet seen is a road as filthy, in wet weather, as that between the railway and the A6.

The A6 is crossed at Hale ("nook of land") and the route then goes into more limestone country with well-wooded hillocks interspersed with rough pasture bounded by the inevitable limestone walls. The winding lanes are popular with horse riders so take care to avoid confrontations with the local cavalry. (You will start to notice blue Lancashire Cycle Way signs about here.) On the only straight stretch you will be lucky enough, if the weather is clear, to gain a surprise view of the Langdale Pikes. (Widdershins riders are advised to stop and look back rather than attempting to peer over their shoulders while still moving forward. The road's too bendy!)

Finally, after more curves and undulations, you break out of wooded country to a view of Arnside across Black Dyke Moss. (There are two possible derivations of the name: some maintain that it is Arnulf's headland or hill, others Arne's saeter, summer sheiling.) Before long you will be crossing the railway and entering the village. Up Briery Bank, down Silverdale Road - and it's the sea! Or, more correctly, the Kent estuary with spectacular views of the Cartmel peninsula and Coniston Old Man and Wetherlam in the background. The estuary supports many bird species throughout the year.

Until quite recently, the village must have been virtually an island, particularly in winter. Arnside and Black Dyke Mosses, and more distantly Hale Moss, would have formed barriers difficult to cross. Gradually, however, it must have become more accessible and many centuries ago it was a departure point for crossing the sands and still is today. Fishing developed later and then salt-making, a vital industry because salting was the only way of preserving meat in pre-refrigeration times. There was not enough fodder to keep livestock through the winter, so autumn was the time for slaughtering and "salting away". There were numerous salt pans for the evaporation of sea water. We shall come upon traces of the salt-making industry all along the Cumbrian coast, usually given away by place names - in Arnside's case by the name

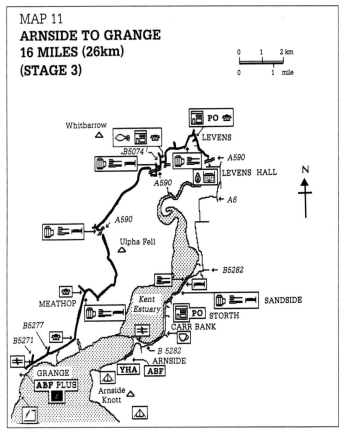

MAP 11
**ARNSIDE TO GRANGE
16 MILES (26km)
(STAGE 3)**

Saltcoates Farm.

Eventually, Arnside became a little port, shipping "marble" from the nearby limestone quarries, but even in the last century there were only a few houses and a coastguard station. It was the completion of the Furness railway in 1857, including the 50-arch, 522 yard viaduct that started the growth of the village as a holiday, retirement and commuting settlement. One remaining link with the past is the 1660 Fighting Cocks Inn; and the old cockpit still exists in the building but, unfortunately, is not open to the public.

The village is left by the Milnthorpe Road, which passes under the railway almost opposite Saltcoates Farm. Between Arnside and Carr Bank you will see trees and an embankment on the left. This carried the Arnside to Kendal railway and also served as an extra sea-dyke. Originally the road went about three-quarters of a mile inland to avoid Arnside Moss. Then the first dyke (visible in the field on the right) was built, which enabled the land to be drained and converted into these flat grass fields.

Past Carr Bank, the road crosses the former railway line and runs beside the River Kent, with good views of the Langdale Pikes. Before the creation of Cumbria in 1974, this part of the estuary used to be known as "Westmorland by the Sea", the only part of that county at the coast. At the Ship Inn, Sandside, the road turns left at what was another of the small River Kent "ports", really no more than a wharf or jetty, and the site of a "cross-channel ferry". At the other end of the straight was another port and the former pub, The Dixies, which still stands as a private house near to the Cottage Restaurant. The importance of this port was emphasised in the eighteenth century when the Milnthorpe-Dixies road became one of the first toll roads in the area. However, the building of the viaduct at Arnside stopped all that.

About half a mile past the Dixies corner the route crosses the River Bela. If you are in no hurry, you might turn right into the grounds of Dallam Tower. This early eighteenth-century house is not open to the public but there is a public road through the gardens from which a herd of roe deer can often be seen. Otherwise turn left just after the bridge, on to the marsh road. The old railway to Kendal veered inland here after crossing the salt marshes at the mouth of the Bela by a viaduct which, together with a bridge over the road,

"Westmorland by the Sea." Sandside from The Dixies Corner

has long since been removed. However, the embankment which led to them still stands high above the roadway. Northward from here, the embankment along the coast is a straightforward sea dyke. The rounded hill near it is a drumlin, as are the higher ones inland towards Heversham. The flat land hereabouts used to be sea bed or salt marsh before the dyke was built and the land drained.

The peace of the marsh road is broken as the route approaches the busy A6. There are asphalt footpaths little used by pedestrians, along which cyclists might prefer to wheel their bikes for the next few hundred yards to Levens Hall. This is open to the public, as is the garden which is famous for having the finest topiary work in Britain. It was laid out in 1692 by James II's French gardener, Beaumont, who also laid out Hampton Court gardens. It was he who planted the half mile avenue of oaks in Levens Park (across the main road). The hall is easily the largest Elizabethan (late sixteenth-century) house in Cumbria, although actually built round a pele tower put up in the days of the Scottish raids some two centuries before. So the raids were a reality even as far south as this. (There are two more peles in the Arnside area but you can't see them from the route.) As optional extras the hall has the odd ghost or two but the owners will not encourage you to hang around until midnight in the hope of seeing one.

Continue along the A6 from Levens Hall, crossing the River Kent. The route underpasses the A590 at a point where the A6 leaves you rather than you leave it. Once under the bridge the main road miraculously transforms itself into a relatively quiet country lane leading into the village of Levens ("Leofa's headland" - between the Kent and the Gilpin rivers). This is limestone country, as you'll see from the field walls and older buildings. Keep straight forward through the village, ignoring side turnings until the next Cycle Way sign. Here, go left past the church down to Causeway Lane on the right. The village pub is just past the junction.

The causeway is part of an ancient pack-horse way across the flat land of Levens Moss in the Lyth valley. This was once covered by the sea and later, as the sea level retreated, the clay of the salt marshes became covered with peat bog. In fact the Furness and Cartmel peninsulas were virtually islands, most easily accessible by the tricky route across the sands of Morecambe Bay. It wasn't until drainage, under the land enclosures towards the end of the eighteenth century, that the water table fell. This enabled the Ulverston-Carnforth Turnpike road to be built in 1818 across this and Haverthwaite Moss further west.

> *Bundles of chats in thousands laid*
> *deep in Haverthwaite Moss*
> *then pinnel and stane, pinnel and stane*
> *to build a way for the hoss.*
>
> *Irvine Hunt*

So a local poet has it in words that give a good picture of road building over the mosses. "Chats" were small branches or twigs on top of which the stones were placed. Then pinnel, coarse gravel, was used to fill in the spaces. As you ride across the Moss you will see the opposite "shore", otherwise the great limestone cliff of Whitbarrow ("white hill") Scar. About a mile along the road, ignoring a side road branching off to the north, you will come to Sampool Bridge which crosses the River Gilpin and will note with some surprise in this relatively unpopulated area a fish and chip shop. Just beyond this is the Gilpin Bridge Hotel.

Past the hotel, it is necessary to cross the main road, the A590. Take care, for the traffic is fast and many drivers are apparently unable to see two-wheeled vehicles. Luckily, it won't be necessary to take your life into your hands and try another swift dash further on to recross the A590. Instead, like the White Rabbit in "Alice's Adventures in Wonderland", you "pop down a large rabbit-hole under the hedge", since the Cycle Way here neatly follows an underpass made for farm animals. This tunnel leads to the old main road, now a peaceful lane beneath the limestone cliffs, but imagine what it was like when it carried the traffic to and from Sellafield, Barrow, and the rest of southwest Cumbria. No wonder the Navy in Barrow used to call it the Ho Chi Minh Trail, after the notorious supply route in Vietnam. In a couple of miles you will come to the Derby Arms, so named because the manor of Witherslack ("wooded valley") was given to the Earl of Derby by Henry VII. After this hostelry, the Cycle Way leads back via another tunnel to the south side of the A590.

The route heads across more reclaimed land, namely Meathop Moss. Again, as happens so often round the flat head of Morecambe Bay (and the tall reeds in the roadside ditches give you a clue), you are riding across the former sea bed. To your left front is Ulpha Fell, previously an island but with a different geology from the limestone you have seen ever since Kirkby Lonsdale and to which you will return shortly.

Ulpha Fell is made of older, darker, slaty and non-limy rock, called mudstone because it came originally from the sea bed millions of years ago and hardened by compression. Massive contortions in the earth's crust in distant times, involving whole blocks of land slipping along fault lines, brought it to the surface here, where it is almost surrounded by the younger limestone. You were on mudstone for the last mile before the Derby Arms, but on Ulpha Fell the bedrock can actually be seen across the fields. Tilted up sharply in rows like the ridges on a dinosaur's back, they make very frustrating country for farming.

The road here is not well drained and you are liable in wet weather to be wheeling a tortuous route between puddles and dodging the muddy patches near field gates. After a mile the road turns right and heads for another "island". The embankment of limestone blocks along the west side of this stretch of road is a sea dyke, at least 200 years old. Long superseded by the bank alongside the present shoreline of the Kent estuary, it now has reclaimed land on both sides. But there have still been floods under exceptional circumstances since the latest embankment was built. Further strengthening is going on as this Guide is going to press. The next "island" sticking up above the old sea bed, limestone again, contains the hamlet of Meathop ("middle plot of enclosed marshland"). Coming ashore here at a T-junction you turn right and cycle up to a farm. Take the left fork which scrapes the gable end of Meathop Hall (late seventeenth century) and heads south down the western side of the hill.

After about a mile, you come to the embankment of the west coast railway. This embankment doubled up as a new sea dyke which allowed large areas of salt marsh to be drained and converted into farmland. The route crosses the River Winster here, near a sluice gate that lets it out beneath the railway to the estuary, except at high tides. This river used to divide the now-defunct county of Westmorland from the detached part of old Lancashire, until it was straightened into its present course during the land reclamation. From that time until the counties became Cumbria in 1974, the boundary kept its original meandering course over the plain, crossing and recrossing the altered river. This must have been frustrating for surveyors, land owners, farmers and others when they found that little bits of one county were on the "wrong" side of the river. The building of the railway led to other changes too. The construction of Arnside viaduct caused the River Kent to move its channel eastward. This led to silting along the western shore which had previously been regularly scoured by river and tides. As a result, Holm Island became linked to the mainland except at high tides. So let's not have any romancing about the unchanging English countryside. The land itself is new along this stretch of the Cycle Way.

The route now follows the railway, past the golf course to the main road at the edge of Grange. One of its fleshpots is the Victorian pile that forms the Cumbria Grand Hotel. Grange was a small village until the Ulverston-Carnforth section of the railway - the last and most difficult bit - was completed in 1857. This made it easy to reach by the growing population of northwest England and the town developed as a quiet, rather genteel resort. Nowadays it is a tourist-cum-commuter-cum-retirement town, a sort of small Harrogate by the sea.

Soon after entering Grange, you pass the railway station on the left and a terrace of shops on the right. In case you think that this is all there is, be of good heart: the main shopping area is a little further on and contains a good mixture of facilities, including a cycle shop on the right as you approach the town centre. However, a word of

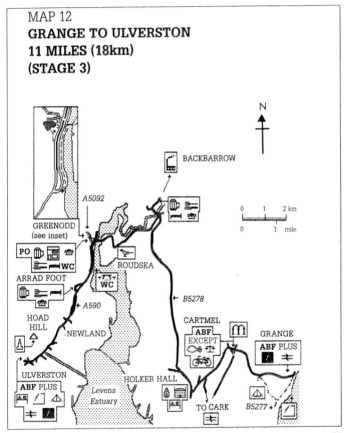

MAP 12
GRANGE TO ULVERSTON
11 MILES (18km)
(STAGE 3)

warning to the thirsty: so genteel is Grange that it has very few pubs. In compensation, when the weather is fine, there are good views across Morecambe Bay from the promenade, including the prominent great blocks of Heysham nuclear power station. The balmy climate of the town is here reflected in the type of shrubs and plants in the gardens and by the senior citizens stepping briskly along. A facility here for the hardy, some might say the foolhardy, is an open-air swimming bath.

The route leaves the town centre via Grange Fell Road up a steep hill. This may be all very well for fanatically fit and experienced cyclists but we weaker brethren, as well as those in search of accommodation, might think of continuing southward, parallel to the sea past the main area of small hotels and guest houses. In three-quarters of a mile a road signposted "Cartmel 2 miles" gives easier gradients, less height to climb, less motor traffic, and also camp sites.

There is further camping at High Fell Gate, on the left just after rejoining the proper route, with a fine view into the broad vale of Cartmel, a continuation of the Windermere valley. Both were once occupied by the same Ice Age glacier. During the later melting, the lower part remained blocked with stagnant ice which dammed the water pouring from the fells, making it overflow into the Backbarrow valley. The lake has drained that way ever since, leaving the Vale of Cartmel with only a little beck. This suited the Augustinian monks, however, who founded Cartmel Priory there in 1188, although it can be a frost hollow in winter. As usual, the cloister was on the sunny side of the main building, but this proved to be a disaster as the ground was too wet and part of it eventually collapsed. There was no alternative but to rebuild it on the cold northern side, so Cartmel was unusual in having its cloister on the side away from the sun, although nothing now remains. The priory church was spared at the Dissolution of the Monasteries because it was also the parish church. No other buildings remain except the gatehouse in the village square.

Several of the gravestones in the churchyard record deaths by drowning while crossing the sands and, in the registers of Cartmel Parish Church alone, 141 people were recorded drowned between 1580 and 1880. An old signpost in the village states that it is fifteen miles to Lancaster and seven miles to Ulverston "OVERSAND", which shows how folk used to risk crossing the estuaries. This is understandable, remembering that the only other way was by causeways at Levens, for Lancaster, or Bouth, for Ulverston. The overland route to Lancaster was originally thirty-six miles, on a packhorse way via Kendal. Even when the Levens Bridge turnpike road was opened in 1818 it was twenty-five miles. From Ulverston to Lancaster the respective distances were forty-one and thirty-five miles, compared with twenty-two miles via the two estuary crossings. It was Cartmel Priory that provided the guides who led travellers across, at least from 1501 to the Dissolution, when the Duchy of Lancaster took over and paid for a guide or "carter", as he is officially called.

There are attractive houses in The Square and Cavendish Street and Cartmel is picturesque enough for the most discerning tourist, despite the strictures of Richard Ayton, writing in 1813: "The town is mean, and laid out with an awkwardness most complete, that despises both appearance and convenience..." (Innes Macleod, ed., *Sailing on Horseback*).

The racecourse, one of the only two in Cumbria (the other is at Carlisle), has two meetings a year and Cartmel is best avoided at that time (spring and summer bank holidays), as it gets extremely busy and accommodation is likely to be unobtainable. An even better reason for being somewhere else is that the Cycle Way actually crosses the racecourse! It then leaves by a gate at the end of the village car park and follows a bridleway through fields and woods to Holker. You'll get one of the best views of the Priory from here, looking back.

We've now passed from limestone to the dark slates and mudstones again. The bedrock pokes out of the ground in places. This is an old road from Cartmel to Holker and on to Ulverston ("oversand" of course). The surface is rough, but only for one field, and at least there is no motor traffic. The field walls alongside the road are made of the local stone and they continue through a plantation at quite a distance apart, showing that it was originally a wide roadway. Bracken and foxgloves indicate that the soil is more acid than that found on the limestone. Not far beyond the wood, those in search of accommodation can divert to the left down a tarred lane to Cark, otherwise there is nothing until Greenodd, eight miles further. At Cark the beck, the Eea (pronounced Ay), which accelerates and shoots down to the sea, powered a cotton mill near The Engine Inn in the eighteenth and nineteenth centuries. The terrace houses on both sides of the beck, plus the two-storey row higher on the south side, were built in the 1780s for mill workers. So Cark was more an industrial village than an agricultural one, although it had a corn mill. There are also traces of a coal wharf where the beck enters the salt marsh and a little port which was used by "flats" - coal vessels in the pre-railway period, before 1857.

For those not wishing to rest their weary heads, the Cycle Way proper continues up the tarred road to the right and over a ridge. On the way down, you come to two mysteries, neither of which the authors have so far solved, plus a surprise. The first mystery is the purpose of a walled rectangular enclosure lacking an entrance, which stands to the right of the road. Immediately following comes the surprise, some signs warning of the presence of adders, but if you've survived to read them you shouldn't have anything to worry about. The second mystery a little further on is a handsome house to the left which bears the apparently insulting name of the Hole of Ellel. Why? Past this point a steep descent brings us to the road at Holker Hall, where the night sleepers of Cark will rejoin the route. Holker Hall, owned by the Duke of Devonshire's family, the Cavendishes, dates from the sixteenth century. The present building is largely Victorian, although in Elizabethan style. It was built in red sandstone, made available via the new railway, and no doubt a status symbol in contrast with the local limestone and slate. Holker Hall has a motor museum and formal and woodland gardens, all open to the public. Beyond Holker the route runs north for almost four miles between the slate Bigland Hills and the flat reclaimed land of the Leven estuary, which soon gives way to birch woods on peat mossland. Where the fields start, glance at the trees beside a lane that branches off to the west. The first ten or so on both sides of this road, with their light coloured foliage, must be a rare sight anywhere in northern Europe, let alone Cumbria: an avenue of walnut trees.

For those interested in industrial archaeology, a diversion at Low Wood to the Backbarrow area is worthwhile. The lowlands fringing the Lake District have always attracted industries which used large quantities of water, because of the many rivers pouring off the rain-soaked fells. In the past, this enormous energy was also useful for driving mill-wheels. Backbarrow had one of the oldest iron furnaces in Britain that was continuously worked. A weir to harness the powerful River Leven was built, together with a bloomery forge, in 1685; and a blast furnace and a refinery operated here from 1711. Charcoal was the main fuel right up to 1926 when coke was used. Upstream, a fulling mill, for cleansing and thickening cloth, pre-dated the ironworks and there were also two cotton mills. One of these began life as a corn mill, was then a paper mill before going over to cotton, and was finally used for producing ultramarine or blue for industrial purposes, including "Reckitt's Blue" for laundering. It closed in 1981 and eventually became part of a time-share complex. The three-storeyed terrace houses at Brow Edge were build to attract cotton spinners in the late eighteenth century, at a time when their skill was in great demand. The charcoal was produced in large quantities in the woodlands of the southern Lake District and kept many people in work. The availability of charcoal also led to the establishment in 1799 of a gunpowder works further downstream at Low Wood.

"Corn mill, did we hear you say? Corn? When the only crop here is grass?" True, but bread is the staff of life and without railways or good roads there used to be no cheap way of transporting flour from drier districts that were more suited to growing corn. So oats used to be grown in abundance, and some wheat, throughout the lowlands of Cumberland and the Furness district of Lancashire until at least the middle of the nineteenth century. This reached its peak during the Napoleonic Wars when the proportion of land under plough seems unbelievable by present-day standards. In wet autumns the harvested grain had to be heat-dried, using peat or wood for fuel, and many corn mills had kilns for this purpose.

At Haverthwaite ("oats clearing" - see what we mean?) Bridge the route slips off to the left along a bridleway on the south bank of the River Leven, passing through the Roudsea Wood National Nature Reserve. This is renowned for its variety of habitats, with former islands of slate and limestone surrounded by sea clays and peat mosses - and a consequent variety of plant and animal life. It was anything but a nature reserve at one time. There was pannage (foraging by pigs), cutting underwood (coppicing) for poles and many other uses, as well as cooperage (barrel-making), wood-turning, and making of coarse matting and swill baskets (from bark). There was also charcoal burning and the extraction, by wood-burning, of potash for soap-making, which supplied the textile industry, especially in Kendal. So what you are passing through is just the leftovers from this past multitude of activities. Wildlife wouldn't get much of a chance here in the good-old-bad-old-days when labour was cheap. And that probably applied to most of the English countryside. You leave the reserve on reaching a former railway track. This ran from Windermere, where it still exists as the much-loved Lakeside and Haverthwaite steam railway, to the Carnforth-Barrow line at Ulverston. The pair of typical railway-company brick houses at Lady Syke are in marked contrast to the tradition of building in local stone. The Cycle Way now continues west to the river itself, which it crosses by a new footbridge at Greenodd ("green promontory"). For widdershins riders this is reached tortuously below the carriageways of the A590 (see inset map). Greenodd was once a busy little port, shipping copper, lead and slate from the Lake District and taking coal in, until the railway altered the river's course, as it did at Grange. The quayside was in front of the Ship Inn (built 1772), which is right up against the former sea cliff behind. Incidentally, if you're planning any two-night stops, Greenodd is well-placed for a trip to Coniston Water.

Now along the A590 for the busiest three miles of the Cycle Way, the road runs along the foot of steep slate hills which contrast sharply with the flat reclaimed estuary land opposite. There's a picnic site overlooking the estuary half a mile to the south. At Newland there used to be a whole complex of industries powered by Newland Beck, including a blacking mill, a corn mill and the first iron blast furnace in the district - another mainly non-agricultural village. The monument on Hoad Hill, a half-scale reproduction of an early Eddystone Lighthouse, was built in 1850 to commemorate Sir John Barrow, geographer and Secretary to the Admiralty. Explorers seeking the Northwest Passage named after him Barrow Point, Alaska and Barrow Inlet in the Canadian North West Territories. Approaching Ulverston ("Ulfr's farmstead") there is a

The monument on The Hoad at Ulverston. Stan Laurel was born quite near to where this photograph was taken

wide but little-used pavement on the west side of the road. Technically it's not for cycles but if you should feel like walking and escaping the traffic for a spell...The chimneys ahead belong to the Glaxochem works, Ulverston's biggest employer.

The town is also Cumbria's main centre for electronics. An underwater technology industry building off-shore oil and gas installations has also been developed, mainly by former employees of Vickers at Barrow. There used to be a blast furnace until the 1930s and Ulverston was once the main port of the estuary. A canal was

63

built when the estuary silted up, Canal Head being on the left as you enter the town. Another main industry used to be brewing, until Hartleys was taken over and the brewing transferred elsewhere. Ulverston is the first market town since Kirkby Lonsdale, and is the agricultural centre for the southern Lake District, Furness, the Millom district and some of the west coast too. The parish church lost its tower in a gale in 1540, so it was rebuilt with six-foot thick walls, using stones from nearby Conishead Priory which was dismantled at the Dissolution of the Monasteries. The northwest window is of painted glass which is resembled only by one other, in Salisbury Cathedral. George Fox, the founder of Quakerism, used to live at Swarthmoor Hall, on the outskirts of the town. Finally, no fans of early cinema comedy should fail to visit the endearing Laural and Hardy Museum (Stan was born at Ulverston), which is behind the fish and chip shop in King Street.

Rampside Hall, with its twelve chimneys

Stage 4
Ulverston to Millom

With the Laurel and Hardy signature tune ringing in your ears, take to the road again joyfully. Leave Ulverston via the Bardsea road from the central roundabout, past the Stan Laurel pub. Our hero was born in Argyle Street, one of the streets opposite; the house has a plaque on the wall. On the left, where you pass under the railway, is a wall of dark slaty rock. This is the last slate you'll see until you reach the West side of the Furness peninsula because you are about to re-enter limestone country. (Don't be deceived by the red sandstone round the bridge itself. It was brought in by rail.) The route passes the Leisure Centre on the left, which includes a swimming bath. Further on, to the right is a camp site, the last before Askam, on the other side of the peninsula.

Beyond, in pleasant countryside, the Cycle Way is at first lined with hedges and limestone walls, then with iron railings as you cross a lovely parkland of mature trees, with a racehorse gallop on the left. After this, also on the left, is Conishead Priory, founded in the twelfth century as a hospital for lepers and others. The present building, a mansion built in 1821 in the Gothic Revival style, became a religious institution again in 1976, this time Tibetan Buddhist. The Manjushri Institute took it over as a centre for religious studies, the inhabitants including both lay and ordained people. It's open to the public on weekends and bank holidays. Here you can turn right into the village of Bardsea ("Beornred's island") if you wish to use its facilities. Widdershins riders can reach Bardsea by taking first left after Sea Wood.

Beyond the park, two lanes on the left lead to the Levens estuary just north of Wadhead Point, where there's a view of Chapel Island. This was on one of the oversand routes across the estuary. Iron ore used to be shipped from this shore in the mid-1800s when the Furness mines were at peak production. The main road reaches the coast a quarter of a mile further south, at Bardsea Country Park, with the all-limestone Victorian church at Bardsea standing proud on the hill opposite. There are tables for picnicking as well as a public convenience, one of several on this coast. Would that all rural areas were so well provided.

After passing a cafe, the road enters Sea Wood which is unusual in having such tall trees at the sea's edge. Not much of Britain's coastline is as sheltered from winds as this. A diversion can be made along a side road to Birkrigg Common with its pre-Roman stone circles. Baycliff offers good views of Morecambe Bay, as well as some facilities. The next village, Aldingham ("settlement of Alda's people"), was once much larger but parts have long been lost to the sea. The church is dedicated to St Cuthbert, which usually means

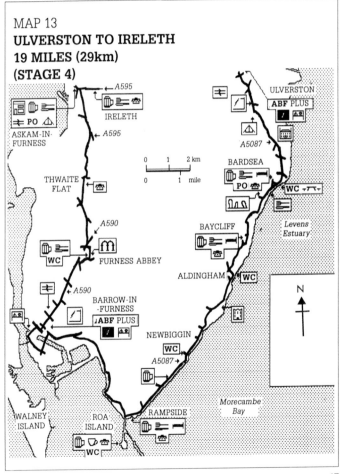

MAP 13
ULVERSTON TO IRELETH
19 MILES (29km)
(STAGE 4)

that his remains (he died in 687) were rested there on their seven-year journey. This was from Lindisfarne in Northumberland to Chester-le-Street in Durham after the Danish invasion of 875. "With map-reading like that it's no wonder it took such a long time" you'll be thinking, but the monks are thought to have been considering taking their precious relics to the greater safety of Ireland. (Their final move was to Durham, in 995.) All villages on this coast were once little ports. Bardsea handled general merchandise as well as iron ore. Baycliff exported iron ore in the eighteenth and nineteenth centuries as did Baycliff Gate Foot, just southwest of Maskel Point. Ore fragments are still said to be seen at places along the shore. Bardsea, Ulverston and Barrow even had a steamer service in the early 1840s, just foreshadowing the arrival of the railways. So these villages, as well as Cark and Newland, unlike the supposedly average English village, had more to do with industry than farming, not to mention fishing. This is typical all round the southern Lake District margin.

The countryside becomes easier here for cyclists, with gentler slopes. The limestone has disappeared beneath a softer red sandstone, which can be seen in a few garden and field walls at Rampside. There are fine views all along this coast in good visibility, across Morecambe Bay to the Lancashire coast, with the Pennines in the background. Heysham nuclear power station and Blackpool Tower are landmarks. For widdershins riders there are views north to the Lake District hills. On the left approaching Rampside a tall tower is a sea mark for guiding vessels into Piel Channel and thus to Barrow. Beyond is Rampside Hall with its twelve chimneys, set diagonally, known as The Twelve Apostles. Rampside ("ram's head" - the supposed shape of the headland) was developed as a bathing resort in the late eighteenth century, the only one south of Maryport, and well before the railway age when most seaside development began. This bit of road, from Aldingham to Rampside, dates from the same period; it isn't on the map of Furness drawn by William Brasier in 1745 (reproduced in B.P.Hindle's book).

The Cycle Way reaches its southernmost point here at the Concle Inn. An interesting diversion continues southwest along a causeway which was built in 1847 to carry a railway to a steamer quay on Roa ("red" - possibly referring to its red sandstone rocks)

The lifeboat station at Roa Island, with Piel Island in the background right

Island. The venture failed. A boat may be taken to Piel Island, with its substantial ruined fourteenth-century castle and (intact) pub; enquire at the café at the end of the ramp. The castle used to be called The Pile ("lofty building") of Fotheray, the fodder island (because of its hay crop). So the name, Piel Castle, has no connection with the pele towers seen elsewhere along the route. Lambert Simnel, the pretender to the throne of Henry VII, landed here in 1487 from Dublin to start his unsuccessful attempt to gain the throne. That now makes two mentions of Ireland. There'll be more as we go round the Cumbrian coast. About halfway along the causeway a gravel spit leads to the left to link up with Foulney ("bird island"), a long low island leased by the Cumbria Wildlife Trust and maintained as part of the South Walney and Piel Channel Flats Site of Special Scientific Interest.

Back at the Concle Inn, named after the tide-washed Concle Bank, a quarter of a mile offshore, the Cycle Way begins its northward course. Along the western side of the Furness peninsula, it follows at first the "Westfield Nature Trail". For half a mile this uses the track of the old Roa causeway railway, now a riot of bracken, willowherb and sallows. It is then diverted sharply towards the coast, to go round the Irish Sea gas terminal. (You will see the offshore rigs on the next Stage if visibility is good.)

The Cycle Way runs for a while parallel to the remains of a typical Cumbrian coast field-boundary. This has a broad foundation of large rounded stones of varied origin, which were carried from the Lake District by Ice Age glaciers and left buried in the boulder clay that remained after the ice had melted. They would be gathered up when the land was cleared for cultivation and heaped into embankments some three feet high, the topsoil having doubtless been removed first. The soil would then be put over the stones and thorn hedges planted in it. You will see such hedges-on-walls many times along the coast. The stones were ground into their present shape during the long journey within the glaciers, so are almost useless for building. See if you can spot the granite rocks as you cycle alongside the old wall. There are no local stones among them, for the local sandstone was too soft to survive the grinding by glaciers. The only hint of the bedrock you might see hereabouts will be the odd russet-coloured ploughed field.

Soon you reach the top of a bracken-covered bluff, with a dramatic view across tidal flats to Roa, Piel Castle, Walney Island and Barrow, with its shipyard cranes. From Westfield Point the Cycle Way swings back to the old railway track and the sands give way to salt marsh near Roosecote ("sheep enclosure belonging to Roose village") power station. Built on the site of an earlier power station, this was opened in 1991 as a private operation. It is Britain's first combined-cycle power station using gas or oil supplies, the gas conveniently coming from the terminal next door. Its output will almost double that of the original, coal-fired power station. Unfortunately, twenty-two pylons will need replacing or strengthening, and made up to twenty feet taller. Note the fine example of 1940s military architecture - a concrete pillbox - guarding the original power station against attack from the sea: a listed building we hope!

You are now entering Barrow, very much by the back entrance, with a disused gas works thrown in to give the place the look of a Monopoly board. The area becomes less derelict after you cross the Lancaster-Barrow railway and ride into Salthouse Road, where you soon join a main road that passes beneath the same railway line. (Widdershins riders fork right off the main road just after passing under the bridge.) For those going clockwise, there's a wall of the local red stone on the left, just past the bridge, which contrasts sharply with one of dark slate around the church opposite, but the rest of the town is almost wholly brick, with slate roofs. The road then goes up a hill and bears right. On the left at this corner are the old offices of the Furness Railway Company.

You will soon reach a large roundabout with a statue of Henry William Schneider, one of the founding fathers of Barrow, which in the middle of the last century was only a small village. Schneider's original interests in the area were in the iron ore mines of Dalton but he went on to found Barrow's iron and steel works in the 1850s and 60s (now closed). This in its turn led to the establishment of shipbuilding, now the dominant industry. Ahead, on the left-hand side, you will see the finest Victorian town hall in the county. The main facilities of the town are in the streets opposite this building.

Otherwise, follow the route of the Cycle Way and turn left at the Schneider statue. You will straight away pass the offices of VSEL (now the official name of Vickers Shipbuilding and Engineering Ltd). The road then crosses a bridge from which, if you look right, you can't fail to see the massive building that enables ships to be built under cover. The shipyard dates from 1871 and has built merchant ships, surface warships and submarines. Current activities are centred on Trident missile-carrying submarines for the Royal Navy. By far the largest employer in Furness, VSEL employed once about 14,000 people, and the industrial health of the district has been largely dependent on the company. However, as a result of defence cuts following the end of the cold war, many jobs are likely to be threatened in the next few years. "What's good for the world is bad for Barrow-in-Furness" (*The Times,* October 1991).

Turning right after some large Scottish-looking tenements, you will pass the shipbuilding parts of VSEL on the left. Further on, after another roundabout is the covered shipyard. Opposite lies an old Victorian repair dock, now the site of the maritime museum, which

Ramsden Square, Barrow-in-Furness, with James Ramsden's statue looking up Abbey Road

tells the story of steel shipbuilding. The road then leads on to yet another roundabout with statue of another of Barrow's founding fathers, the Duke of Devonshire, owner of Holker Hall as well as much of the land on which Barrow was built. Further on, the route turns left and leads to the last roundabout and - guess what - another statue. This is of James Ramsden, general manager of the Furness Railway Company and the leading light in the planning and development of the town.

You are now at the focal point of this drawing-board-planned town. Ahead lies broad Abbey Road, with the library and museum and to the right lies Duke Street with the town hall. Originally, it was intended that Barrow should grow into an important city but the town's isolation limited growth (a familiar tale in Cumbria). These two roads are what remains of a typically Victorian aspiration. But Barrow did grow dramatically in the early stages: between 1861 and

Outside The Dock maritime museum, Barrow-in-Furness.
The ship on the right, the Emily Barratt, was launched in Millom in 1913.
It is the last commercial schooner to be built in England and is to be restored

1886, the population rose from 2,135 to 47,259.

On the left, behind the public buildings, you will see rows of privately owned terraced housing, another feature of Barrow's history. Much of the housing was originally built and let by Vickers, who subsequently sold it off as private housing, so Barrow has much less council housing than could be expected in an industrial town. To the right lies the shopping centre based on Dalton Road. An old, unplanned through route was cleverly merged into the gridiron layout, though it still kept a less formal character. Much of it was of traditional shops with housing above but these are being replaced by purpose-built stores and much of the road is being pedestrianised. Beyond the town centre, Abbey Road retains its width, and its busy traffic, but becomes a pleasant residential highway. After the railway station there's a public park, followed immediately by Park Drive. Barrow Leisure Centre, which includes modern swimming baths, is quarter of a mile down this road.

Two miles from the town centre, opposite Furness Hospital, Rating Lane slips away on the right towards the magnificent warm-coloured sandstone ruin of Furness Abbey. In its sheltered well-treed valley, this is one of the finest ruins of England according to Pevsner, and is easily the most distinguished building alongside the Cycle Way. This Cistercian foundation had a strong influence on the medieval life. It had farms in Furness, Eskdale and Wasdale, wool being exported as far afield as the Low Countries. It promoted the early iron and steel industry, whose need for charcoal led to so much woodland being retained in South Cumbria when many areas were being deforested. In addition to its own influence, Furness was responsible for the establishment of Calder Abbey in West Cumbria. It was so rich that Robert the Bruce, the man who re-established Scotland's ancient right to self-rule, rode down the coast and raided it. Working on a "nice place you've got here, wouldn't want to see it spoiled would you?" basis he got what he wanted. This included, significantly, a load of iron ore. What's more he didn't spoil the place. That was done by Henry VIII more than 200 years later, when he dissolved the monasteries.

The Cycle Way goes through the grounds and then returns to the busy A590, which you must cross and then turn off left almost immediately into Breast Mill Beck Road, at a red sandstone horse trough dated 1873. (Those needing accommodation are advised to continue along the A590 to Dalton because there isn't much between here and Broughton-in-Furness.) At Thwaite, the route goes off to the right, down Hawthwaite Lane to a railway level crossing. You are now back on limestone but it differs from that in Arnside, Grange and Gleaston because it contained deposits of high-grade iron ore, hematite, which have now been exhausted. There are many abandoned mines and quarries, some now forming the meres which can be seen around Thwaite Flat. Once over the level crossing at Thwaite the Cycle Way leaves the road and slips off along a lane to the left. The sign "Private Road" at Park Farm is true but there is a right of way. This is a deer farm and you will very likely see them in high-fenced paddocks, often sharing the grazing with wild geese that come inland for a quick nibble when high tides cover the marshes. The Cycle Way returns eventually to the road near a brickworks.

Soon, the village of Askam-in-Furness appears on the other side of the railway. It owes its origin in the third quarter of the nineteenth century to a thriving iron and steel works owned by the Millom and Askam Hematite Iron Company (of which more later). The iron works closed at the end of World War I, although it wasn't demolished until 1938. Nothing remains except some terraces of

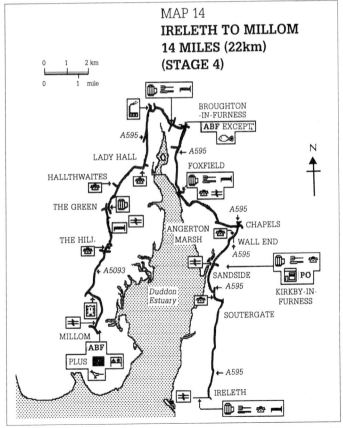

MAP 14
IRELETH TO MILLOM
14 MILES (22km)
(STAGE 4)

former company houses. Fortunately, K Shoes of Kendal opened a branch here in the 1960s, so Askam still keeps some employment. The Cycle Way doesn't go into Askam, so you'll have to cross the railway if you want supplies or the campsite. Ireleth ("hill-slope of the Irishmen"), the original settlement before Askam was created, has few facilities, and is now largely a commuter village with much recent new housing.

Beyond Ireleth, note the absence of trees on this exposed coast in contrast to Conishead and Bardsea on the eastern side of the peninsula. Ireleth Marsh used to be the setting-off point for crossing the Duddon estuary, not only on foot but by coach and horses too. As with the other estuaries, the route was marked by clumps of broom stuck in the sand. Although the estuary is much smaller than Morecambe Bay or the Solway Firth, its sands are no less dangerous. And they have something that the bigger estuaries do not have - immortality in the poetry of Norman Nicholson who lived and died at Millom. To quote *The Times* again, his obituary, in 1987, described him as "the most gifted English Christian provincial poet of his century". Nicholson felt intensely that the nature of his birthplace was important to the understanding of his work; you feel the rocks and fells, the marshes and sands come to life:

> Thigh deep in fresh water
> I waded the channel
> Before the ebb turned.
> Do not ask where
> Foot first stepped astray
> From turf to mud,
> From dry sand to quicksand;

At Ireleth the limestone gives way to the dark slates that you last saw at Ulverston, as you return to the northern part of the peninsula. The field boundaries however are mostly thorn hedges until Soutergate, the first of several small villages that together form Kirkby-in-Furness. The name suggests a Scandinavian settlement. Originally farming, fishing and slate-quarrying villages, Soutergate and Sandside, especially, have become dormitory suburbs of Barrow, hence the shut-down shops near the railway station. Although there are no facilities on the Cycle Way here, if you go up the steep hill on the right, opposite the station, there are two pubs, a post office, a phone box and a general store.

Surprisingly, there have been wrestling matches recently in Kirkby of all places - between some citizens and their consciences. It cannot be easy to support greater use of renewable resources, such as wind and tides, for generating electricity while at the same time welcoming it in your own backyard. At the time of writing there are proposals to build wind-driven generators on Kirkby Moor and a tide-power barrage across the Duddon Estuary.

The Cycle Way rejoins the A595 opposite the magnificent sixteenth- or early seventeenth-century Kirkby Hall. This, like a superb period house in Cark, is ignored by Pevsner while Victorian buildings are fashionably gloated upon. (Note that the caravan site just south of the road junction, which has both tent and caravan symbols on the Ordnance Survey 1:50,000 scale map, does not accept tents, 1992.) Waste heaps on the hillside are from the slate quarries which have provided many jobs in the past and, in the case of the Burlington Slate Company, still do. From Chapels, the Cycle Way follows a narrow sunken lane between fern-and-bramble-clad stone walls upon which thorn hedges grow. Large horizontal trunk-like branches near the base of the hedges result from hedge laying long ago. This lane has an ancient stone-paved surface, as you will notice only too well by its bumpiness. It may be an old road from the slate quarries down to a loading point on the shore.

There is now a one-and-a-half-mile flat stretch along a very quiet road which leads across reclaimed marshland, with ex-islands rising up here and there. Reeds at the roadside mark the start of the old sea-bed, 100 yards before a bridge over a tidal gully known as Kirkby Pool. Waltham Hill is a former island of slate rock where a farmhouse and buildings stand high and dry above the reclaimed land. The rock has been quarried, not only for building the farmstead but possibly also to make the causeway which carries the next stretch of road across a heathy raised peat moss with birch trees, although it may have been made solely with brushwood. This may well be the least frequented part of the entire Cycle Way. Cross the railway at an unmanned crossing. (It's your life, so take care!) There's another farm, Angerton, on a bigger ex-island away to the left. For 200 yards, after crossing another tidal inlet, you're on the

The square in Broughton-in-Furness

seaward side of the railway embankment which here, as at places near Arnside and Grange, also serves as a sea wall. So, if a spring tide is roaring in, keep pedalling!

Another level crossing, manned this time but with bike-accepting side gates (watch out again for trains), returns you to the A595 at Foxfield, only one and a half miles from Broughton-in-Furness ("place beside a brook"). This large village - the Anglian name suggests it was there before the Vikings came - was formerly an important market centre, and still has a weekly market and a good variety of facilities for its size. It is an attractive place, particularly the market square which comes complete with stocks, so behave yourselves.

There is a steep, but pointless, climb out of Broughton to the High Cross Inn. Pointless because you immediately go steeply downhill again, almost to sea level to cross the reclaimed estuary of the River Lickle. Don't waste any praise on this sluggish stream, however, because in another half mile there's a real river, the Duddon. One of Lakeland's best, it tumbles out of its valley here and immediately becomes a tidal watercourse. At Duddon Bridge you are nearer to the Lake District heartland than at any other point on the Cumbria Cycle Way, except Ravenglass. So, if you have time and energy to go up Dunnerdale do so, although there are steep ascents. This valley is the wrong way round, widest at the top end and narrowest here, where it ends abruptly. It is so narrow in fact that the road has to climb the valley side to get in; hence the gruelling gradients. In any case, you have perhaps been puffing enough lately.

At Duddon Bridge, you pass into the old county of Cumberland from what was Lancashire up to 1974. To the right just after the bridge is a road marked "Unsuitable for caravans". This is not on the Cycle Way but a few yards along it to the left are the remains of the old Duddon iron furnace, which was charcoal fuelled. Unfortunately, there's no access but they are visible from the road and from a bridle

Duddon Forge

path that runs past the site. They are one of the few examples of industrial archaeology near to the Cycle Way.

After three-quarters of a mile of steady ascent the route slopes off to the left, down a quiet road which is a relief from the busy A595, with good views to the estuary and to Kirkby Moor beyond. Then it goes through the hamlets of Lady Hall and Hallthwaites to rejoin the main Millom road at The Green, a small village. One last ascent to The Hill, another village, and then it's downhill to Millom, past many road cuttings through lavas and other volcanic rocks (they are also sticking up in the fields).

Millom ("at the mills") Castle, a former home of the Huddlestone family, is incorporated in a working farm on the outskirts of the town, but began life as a pele tower. So, Scottish raiders were feared even at this distance from the Border - and nearly at the end of a peninsula, on the road to nowhere but the sea. Rightly so, as when Robert the Bruce made his raid on Furness Abbey, he came by the coast and across the Duddon Sands, presumably with a guide across these, whether willing or not.

Before Millom was built (and it's not on the 1869 OS map) there was only the village of Holborn Hill, on the high land northwest of the present railway, plus the castle and the superb old church next door. The New Town, as it was called, was constructed southeast of the railway, defying the local geology in that all the building materials were brought in from outside: bricks for the houses, red sandstone for the bigger buildings, and the universal roofing slates. The town was built in the second half of the nineteenth century to house workers employed in the Hodbarrow hematite mines, which were opened in 1855, and in the associated iron and steel works, which first produced iron in 1867. The original owners intended to build their blast furnaces at Mirehouse, south of Whitehaven, but failed to reach agreement with Lord Lowther, the landowner. The company amalgamated with the one owning Askam Ironworks in 1890 to form the Millom and Askam Hematite Iron Company. Hodbarrow was one of the richest iron ore mines in the world. The mine being next to the sea, the water had to be kept out by a sea wall, built in 1890. This was replaced by the one-and-a-half-mile embankment stretching from Hodbarrow Point to Haverigg, but the mine is flooded now. It's worth cycling the one and a half miles

The Friends Meeting House, Brigflatts
Cartmel Priory, early morning

St Cuthbert's Church, Aldingham
Holy Trinity Church, Millom (with castle in background)

to Hodbarrow Point where hematite can be seen quite clearly as deep red streaks within the limestone. The lagoon and much of the derelict land marking the site of the iron industry are now a nature reserve.

The mines and ironworks survived until 1968. After they closed, most of the workers found employment at more distant places such as Vickers in Barrow or British Nuclear Fuels at Sellafield. There is little reminder now of the past, except what is to be seen in the excellent Folk Museum which includes a reproduction of an iron mine, using equipment salvaged from Hodbarrow. Down the street to the left as you approach the library, is a blue plaque above a shopfront, in memory of Norman Nicholson who lived and died in Millom. There's a bust in the library, lifelike enough to enable one of us to cherish an abiding memory of him, shopping bag in hand, on a Millom street.

Norman Nicholson's house, Millom

The sands at Haverigg

Stage 5
Millom to Whitehaven

This section follows the Irish Sea coast, in contrast to the sheltered estuaries of Morecambe Bay and the Duddon. It begins by going to Haverigg ("oats ridge"), past new industries established in the old tannery buildings. Here at last is a firm sandy beach, after the treacherous mud of the estuaries. Here also are dunes that give shelter from westerly winds - and the next place where you'll find that is miles to the north beside the Solway Firth, but that's muddy again. Yet a third benefit, and at Haverigg only, is a south aspect. But people do not throng here to take advantage of this unique combination - it's too remote, although there was an attempt to develop a resort here when the railway came to Millom. Nor are there enough people living nearby to overcrowd the beach on a summer's day. Leisure activities include sailing, when the tide is in, and water skiing on the iron-mine lagoon, to the east. Haverigg has some colour-washed houses reminiscent of Scotland. You'll also notice a new kind of stone wall here, which is confined to a one-and-a-half-mile strip along the Irish Sea coast. It is made of large cobbles, gathered from the shore and rounded by glaciers moving into the Irish Sea lowland from Scotland and the Lake District. The many different sorts of rock - granites, lavas, slates included - make unique and very attractive walls, usually with courses of thin slate.

You now move northward through a more windswept landscape, open to the sea. Between Haverigg and Kirksanton, is the site of another proposed wind-farm to take advantage of the wind. At the time of writing, it had just received planning permission. Beyond, Kirksanton has a village green - not as generous as those we saw along the Pennine footslopes, but they are rarely seen at all in these parts. There's no church, in spite of the name, but send up a prayer for a following wind. One or two standing stones, marked on some maps, are in the fields near the level crossing but are not easily seen. From Silecroft a road runs to the shore - a worthwhile diversion, for the Cycle Way doesn't reach the coast for another seven miles at Eskmeals. The excellent beach at Haverigg extends right round to here and beyond (six miles of it), before becoming boulder-covered. A stiff breeze here can cover the car park - and the field beyond it - with white spume. After Silecroft the Cycle Way rejoins the A595 - but there is less traffic here. Also the road is straighter and wider, so you can enjoy looking at the steep flanks of Black Combe, covered in gorse and bracken. This lump of slate, which towers 1,970 feet above the coast, brews up quite violent weather and often has a cloud cap when the Lakeland fells are clear. Out at sea, to the south-southwest, are the rigs of the Morecambe Bay gasfield and, on a clear day, the Isle of Man can be seen to the west.

Bootle is the capital of the coastal lowland beyond Black Combe.

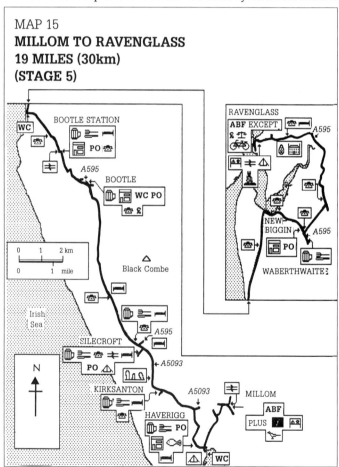

MAP 15
MILLOM TO RAVENGLASS
19 MILES (30km)
(STAGE 5)

Silecroft with Black Combe in the background

Theoretically it is England's smallest market town, receiving its charter in 1347, but the market is extinct now. The name (not unknown to Liverpudlians!) is from "booth", Anglo-Saxon for a dwelling house. Always isolated - even during the road transport boom years of the late eighteenth and early nineteenth centuries the toll roads never penetrated south of Egremont - the village still gives an air of self-sufficiency with a supermarket, butcher and two banks, but meals and accommodation are difficult to find. The old village school, bearing the evocative name of Captain Shaw's and still in use, has a carved red sandstone tablet on its north wall. Dated 1830, it carries texts from the Old Testament including: "Train up a child in the way he should go, and when he is old he will not depart from it." The Cycle Way leaves the A595 here to follow a narrow road that winds between hedges to Bootle Station. Some of the hedges are growing on low stone walls, as is common along the coast. There are various facilities at Bootle Station including accommodation, also more of the elaborate and eye-catching house and garden walls first seen at Haverigg.

The beach cobblestones were in great demand outside the

district too. They used to be loaded on to ships, to such an extent that the tide eventually started eroding the coast. This put the parish to considerable expense. In 1838, three vessels arrived at Annaside near here to load cobbles for Liverpool, perhaps to be used as ballast. Thirty-six local men gathered to resist them, "each carrying a good sprig of oak" (*Whitehaven News*). The ensuing battle resulted in "broken heads and bruised bodies" and the enemy, including women using "frightful" language, finally withdrew. There is now a by-law making it illegal to take stones from the beaches for rock gardens, nowadays their only perceived use, and the language has improved. Hopefully the locals involved in this fracas were too old to have been former pupils of Captain Shaw.

Cycling on from Bootle Station, the road becomes wider and straighter. Ahead, you may hear sounds of battle, not emanating from "sprigs of oak" but from heavy artillery. This is because, on reaching the coast at Eskmeals ("Esk dunes"), the Cycle Way passes through the Ministry of Defence Proof and Experimental Establishment, where shells are fired out to sea. This establishment undertakes full trials of weapons under development (the "Experimental" part of the title) and ensures that the production standards of existing weapons are maintained ("Proof"). Red flags indicate that the range is active and that firing will take place, in which case be prepared for sudden loud bangs. Eskmeals may be noisy at times but it provides welcome jobs in an area that's over-dependent on Sellafield for employment. The landscape is rather bleak behind this establishment, the farmland having wire-fencing rather than the usual thorn hedges or dry-stone walls, but a jagged horizon of sand dunes makes a contrast eventually as you approach the estuary of the River Esk. The dunes also made a home for Stone Age man as he followed the northward retreating ice. He left many of his artefacts round here (and indeed on all of this coastal plain), indicating that the original route by which man came to West Cumbria was probably our old friend, the "oversand" route via Furness. Indeed, with the inland areas heavily forested and marshy, this would be the best way.

At the Esk, the Cycle Way turns inland, beneath the railway. From just to the west of this point the old road used to cross the estuary straight to Ravenglass. However, our route goes along the tide-washed road across a salt marsh, to yet another Newbiggin. A lane going off here northeastward not only reduces your next bout on the A595 but also takes you past Waberthwaite church, a squat little building now closed but in a beautiful position on a low promontory overlooking the estuary. Up to 1844 the rector held Muncaster also and would adjust the time, and length, of morning service, to allow him to cross at low tide to officiate in his other church. For those determined to follow the Cycle Way, and for Cumberland sausage fanatics, the route continues between hedges growing on earth-and-stone baulks to Waberthwaite. Here is the home of Woodhall's pork products, which are exported all over the world. If you are self-catering, pop into their shop and sample some of their produce; alternatively, eat the sausages at the Brown Cow Inn, only 200 yards southward along the A595. Waberthwaite itself is a scattered settlement two miles long, most of it just off the main road, very sensibly.

Unfortunately, there are now three and a half winding miles of the A595 to negotiate. This is the only way to cross the Esk, still tidal here, and to pass round the end of Muncaster Fell's granite ridge. The flat area to the north and south of the bridge is the bed of a former tidal inlet. Until recently, it would have been a marshy place, probably covered in alder trees. It was probably almost impassable before being cleared, drained and causewayed during the Enclosures. This is why the old road took the oversand route across both the Esk and the River Mite, to the north of Muncaster Fell, where there is a similar area. At the end of the flat stretch the road makes a right-angled turn to the left and begins to climb the flank of Muncaster Fell. On this corner, a bridle path leading off to the right follows the line of the old Roman road, which, skirting the marshy land to the south, led from the fort at Ravenglass up Eskdale to Hardknott Fort and, eventually, Ambleside. South of this road no traces of Roman occupation have been found: they seem to have been content to leave the inhabitants in peace.

The landscape is as sheltered here as it was exposed beside the coast. The Cycle Way goes through the grounds of Muncaster Castle, West Cumbria's only stately home open to the public. Trees have been planted here and allowed to grow to maturity, resulting in magnificent parkland, more extensive and scenic than any met with elsewhere on the Cycle Way. Most of the present "castle" was built in the 1860s, incorporating parts of a medieval castle, which itself began as a pele tower, probably completed in 1242. In that year the Penningtons moved in from the Furness area (there's a village called Pennington near Ulverston). And they are still at Muncaster! After 750 years, they must be getting quite used to the place. The house and gardens are open to the public and there is an aviary in the grounds.

"Caster", in the name Muncaster, refers to the southernmost of a long line of Roman forts stretching from the Solway Firth, as seaward defences to prevent Hadrian's Wall from being out-flanked. However, unlike the others, the fort at Ravenglass, called Glannoventa, faced landwards not seawards and so may have been designed to protect the port from the local inhabitants rather than from sea-borne invaders. Much of the fort was destroyed when the West coast railway was built in the middle of the last century. However, along the road that passes the camp site between Ravenglass and the Castle, is a Roman bathhouse, a remarkably well-preserved building with walls over twelve feet high.

Ravenglass, being a tourist place, has a variety of facilities. It was a market town and a port, but now it is neither. The market served a small and poor area as well as being in competition with Bootle, and expired in the nineteenth century. So did the port, which had to face competition from newer ports such as Whitehaven and Workington. Now it is silted up and has only leisure craft and a few fishing boats. There is only one street, but a charming one. This is as hard to reconcile with the impressions of that stern critic Robert Ayton in 1813 as were his comments on Cartmel: "On the border of this dismal waste stands Ravenglass, a dirty, ragged, forlorn looking town, which, considered in all its relations, in its wretchedness, and the dreariness of its situation, may be pronounced to be the most miserable place, with the title of town, in the kingdom." Has it really changed so much or have our ideas of what is, and is not, picturesque?

If you plan a stopover in Ravenglass or saddle-soreness compels it, consider a ride on the narrow gauge railway through delightful scenery to Eskdale. Formerly a mineral line, its history is shown in a museum at the station. Ravenglass is where the Lake District hills reach nearest to the sea and the line provides the best route from the

At Ravenglass some of the houses back onto the harbour

Cycle Way into the heart of these fells. If not saddle-sore but with a day to spare, consider a trip to Wast Water, one of the finest lakes.

You leave Ravenglass via a path on the railway bridge, which stands close to the spot where the original coast road forded the River Mite. This is the fifth and last of the fordable estuaries. John Wesley (remember his sarcasm at Appleby?) crossed four of them on a journey from Flookburgh to Whitehaven in 1759. He complained about being misinformed about the tides at all of them by the local inhabitants, "who detain all strangers as long as they can for their own gain or their neighbours". He recommended the traveller to go via Keswick instead, "often in less time, always with less expense, and for less trial of his patience".

A line of dunes stands out dramatically to the west, part of the Drigg Nature Reserve, of which more later. On the north side of the Mite at Saltcoats, another name with saltpan connections, there is a fine wall of cobbles with slate courses, capped with red sandstone.

The Cycle Way follows a quiet road, via a level crossing to the A595, for a mile to Holmrook ("almost-an-island at a river bend"). This village has a main street built-up mostly on one side only. The other gives attractive views across the meadows of the River Irt. The red sandstone bedrock of these parts is largely covered by glacial drift. The stone must have been quarried in the past, for it is quite a

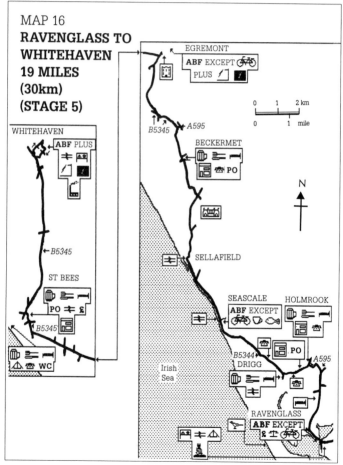

common building material from Holmrook northward. The village has some facilities and the filling station has a well-stocked shop. After Ravenglass, Holmrook is the next and last good point from which to make a day's excursion into Wasdale and/or Eskdale.

At Holmrook, the Cycle Way leaves the A595 again, this time for good, and heads for the coast once more. Sure enough at Drigg, one and a quarter miles from the shore, cobbled walls reappear. The dunes opposite Ravenglass are accessible from here, down a lane to the left. The furthest part is the Drigg Nature Reserve, with a nesting population of 12,000 black-headed gulls. So cover your own noddle lest you should become white-headed. The same lane also leads to a British Nuclear Fuels dump for low-level radio active waste.

Nearness to the shore means more wind, made worse along the road to Seascale ("hut by the sea") by particularly low-cut hedges. At Seascale itself the route reaches the shore. This embryo holiday resort was created in Victorian times by the Furness Railway Company, but the original design was never fulfilled, because of low demand at this remote spot. There is a variety of facilities including plenty of accommodation, which will become increasingly scarce further north. The Cycle Way leaves the road where the latter passes under the railway and follows a track between the railway and the sea. If a strong offshore wind is blowing, this part of the route can, at the least, be described as bracing. It starts as a gravel path but, where it crosses the River Calder by way of the railway bridge, it becomes smooth concrete.

In case you have failed to notice as you approach Sellafield railway station, there is a large industrial complex over the fence. This is the famous British Nuclear Fuels Sellafield. The expression, "You can't miss it", was never more true. The first part is Calder Hall, the world's first industrial-scale nuclear power station. Next comes the nuclear fuel reprocessing plant where uranium fuel rods, which have been used to produce electricity in a nuclear reactor, are treated to separate residual uranium and the by-product plutonium. Highly-active waste is also separated for safe (we hope) storage. A massive new complex to reprocess used fuel from the more modern nuclear power stations is being completed at the time of writing, and a large number of local workers will become unemployed as a result. The used fuel will be brought in by sea to Barrow and then

The Visitors Centre at Sellafield

by rail. At Sellafield station, the Cycle Way turns inland again, along one of the main access roads from the BNF complex (if it's a time when the shifts are changing stand well back until the dust settles). The wind that clipped the hedges may help you up the hill to a roundabout. A 300-yard diversion to the right from here, to the Visitors Centre, is well worth it, even if you're an opponent of nuclear power. It's the most visited place in Cumbria (by locals as much as tourists) and, as well as the exhibition, it has a good café.

Back at the roundabout the Cycle Way slips through a small gate to peace and tranquillity, along a now-superseded road. Gorse hedges grow on stone-and-earth baulks and to the east, if it's clear, there's a superb view of England's highest point, Scafell Pike, with Sca Fell, slightly lower to the right, beyond a sharp cleft called Mickledore. This is the best view of the Lakeland fells from anywhere along the Cycle Way. Incidentally, as though Sellafield wasn't enough, this part of Cumbria suffered a double visitation of the Chernobyl cloud. The wind changed at a critical moment and blew it back over.

At Beckermet, pronounced with the stress on the "er" because it meant the beck of the hermit, the red sandstone is prominent in walls and some buildings. Although it gives the appearance of the traditional English agricultural village, it was until recently within the West Cumbria iron ore mining area. Beckermet Mine was the last in Cumbria to close, as recently as 1980. To the north there is a treeless stretch, although this district was wooded down to the sea until the seventeenth century. Disused iron-mine tracks are much in evidence. Trees reappear beyond the bridge across the River Ehen and at one spot form an arch over the road. The Cycle Way just crosses iron-bearing limestone, beneath glacial drift, between here and Egremont. Although the farm buildings at Pickett How are of red sandstone, across the road are the remains of a hematite mine which must be in limestone.

The Cycle Way strikes westward from Egremont at a junction almost opposite to the castle, without entering the town centre. There's a good variety of facilities and the town is also the best point from which to make a trip into Ennerdale, well worth it if you can spare a day. This is different from all other Lake District dales with its lake at the mouth of the valley, its wooded slopes and its Forestry Commission track in the upper valley, usable by local vehicles and bicycles. Egremont became the local capital when the Barony of Copeland was given to William de Meschines in the early twelfth century. It didn't just grow, like the average market town, but was planned and developed by the lords of the manor in the twelfth and thirteenth centuries, as Appleby was. It received a market charter and remained the trading centre until the nineteenth century when iron ore mining developed. The town has recently gained a new function, as one of Sellafield's dormitory settlements. It has a fine main street, marred by an over-wide gap in its east side, apparently inflicted by the local authority when the land behind was redeveloped. The main tourist attraction is the Crab Fair, held on the third Saturday in September. The name has no connection with the fishing industry but refers to the crab apples with which the public are for some reason pelted during the parade. The Fair has many attractions of which the most famous is the "gurning" competition where the participants put their faces through a horse collar and try to pull the ugliest face.

From Egremont take the road to St Bees. This is steep at first and crosses windswept and relatively high land. Low hedges afford views to the Lakeland fells and the Isle of Man. The straight road and the rectangular fields look as though they were planned on a drawing board. And so they probably were, for this is the classic pattern of the land enclosures made in the eighteenth and early nineteenth centuries. There was a great boost to agriculture nationally at that time, caused by a growth in trade in coal, iron and textiles and in the urban population. There were improved techniques in farming; and the Napoleonic wars also raised the demand for farm produce, with the result that many thousands of acres were enclosed, especially between about 1795 and 1830. Productivity improved and the landscape changed completely. This is free draining land, which is at a premium in a fairly wet climate. Its disadvantage, delaying its enclosure for more up-to-date farming methods, is exposure to the wind.

Down a steep hill, with views to St Bees Head and still more rectangular fields, is St Bees village. Red sandstone is much in evidence here, in the buildings and in the magnificent cliffs, the only ones in Cumbria. Bird watchers with time to spare could have a rewarding day here. The Head is also the start of Wainwright's Coast-to-Coast path, first met at Kirkby Stephen. Here, it heads north for a mile or two, before turning inland towards the distant east coast.

This is England's nearest point to Ireland and it is reputedly named after Bega, an Irish princess who fled here to avoid marriage and established a nunnery - a legend perhaps but there certainly was a nunnery. And there's a strong Irish connection in history from here northward, as you shall see. The nunnery church, St Mary and St Bega, has survived. Pevsner describes it as "gratifyingly complete", which from him is praise indeed. There's also a well-known public school.

The Cycle Way reaches its westernmost point at St Bees and then turns north, for otherwise you would get very wet. A long, stiff climb along the Whitehaven road brings the western fells into view on the right, and Albright and Wilson's chemical works on the left. This produces raw materials, intermediate and finished products, mainly for the detergents and toiletries industries; it also serves the rubber, plastics, textile and paint industries. A rectangular field pattern indicates late enclosure again on this exposed land. On the descent into Whitehaven, Criffel may be seen - a massive lump in Scotland - beckoning us forward to the next section of the Cycle Way. Just south of Whitehaven, you leave the orange-red sandstone, used so much for buildings, particularly at Seascale and St Bees. You are now on a coalfield that extends to Maryport, though the last colliery, Haig Pit, on the clifftop to the north of Albright and Wilson's, closed in the mid 1950s. Even so, this didn't mark the end of Cumbrian coal mining, because a private drift mine (one driven horizontally into the hillside) recently opened in the valley to the right.

The Lowthers, the local landowners, although themselves living in Westmorland, began to expand the mining of coal in the seventeenth century. Being near the sea, the coal was easily got to ships, which could then take it to distant markets, mainly Ireland at first and, later, America. (The earliest toll roads in Cumbria were in this area to enable the coal to be transported to Whitehaven. You have just ridden along one of them from St Bees.) The ships brought back many cargoes, but especially tobacco which was loaded in Virginia after unloading African slaves there. By the eighteenth century Whitehaven was England's third most important port, after London and Bristol. So the town prospered and the Lowthers became the Earls of Lonsdale who laid out Whitehaven as a new town, described by Pevsner as "the earliest post-medieval planned town in England". However there is a small area of pre-Georgian streets around the present site of the Tourist Information Office. With its Georgian buildings, this area bears a marked similarity to one of its main customers, Dublin, and indeed the prosperity of the latter led to that of the other. During the twentieth century, with the decline of iron and coal mining, as well as iron and steel manufacture, the town went into a decline like the rest of West Cumbria, until new industries came in, such as Albright and Wilson and of course BNF. Collaboration between the local authorities, the development agencies and BNF itself has led to a renovation of Georgian buildings.

Whitehaven might have got its name from the colour of the cliffs next to the harbour. Seen from the sea these may have appeared pale, in contrast to the red cliffs of St Bees to the south. The town's history is well illustrated in the museum in the Civic Centre.

Clockwise riders will have to cycle past their turn-off point and go on to the widdershins route to reach it, because of one-way streets. Similarly, widdershins riders will have to go past their turn-off if they want to see the harbour. On the south side of the harbour two features of the town's history are visible. (Turn left just as you enter the town centre if you want to see them or, in the case of widdershins riders, go straight across the road when leaving the town centre instead of turning left for St Bees.) The first is the old entrance to the long-closed Wellington Pit. The second, when you reach the cliff top, is one of the guns that were spiked by the famous John Paul Jones when he raided Whitehaven in 1788, during the American War of Independence. Despite his Welsh-sounding name and being a commander in the American Navy, Jones was a Scot, born just across the water in a village at the foot of Criffel, the mountain you might have seen as you came down the hill into town. No doubt he was glad to have the opportunity to put one over the "auld enemy",

but the raid wasn't very successful. His memory is better preserved as the name of an old-time dance, probably American originally. But they are unlikely to dance in his memory in Africa because, before his naval career, he made his money from the slave trade. And guess where he first operated from, in

The Candlestick Chimney at William Pit, Whitehaven

At Haverigg (Photo courtesy of Cumbria County Council)
Silloth

*Above: Between Allonby
and Silloth
(Photo courtesy of
Cumbria County Council)*

*Right:
St Mary's Church,
Abbeytown, all that
remains of Holm
Outram Abbey*

The entrance to Whitehaven Harbour.
The Scottish mountain, Criffel, is just to the right of centre

that lucrative business, Whitehaven!

Another John had a mixed reception at the town earlier in the eighteenth century. John Wesley, who you will remember felt he was being conned at the various estuary crossings round the coast, had already preached at Whitehaven eight years previously, in 1751. "A few stones were thrown at first", he wrote in his *Journal,* "But the bulk of the congregation was deeply serious". However Whitehaven is likely to have a more friendly greeting for you and it has the best variety of facilities since Barrow-in-Furness. And there is a first-class bookshop, both new and second-hand, in the town centre: just ask for Moon's in Roper Street.

The ruins of Workington Hall

Stage 6
Whitehaven to Silloth

The route leaves Whitehaven by the area known as North Shore. To the west of the railway, adjacent to Bransty Station, was the site of Whitehaven's only ironworks. The Lonsdale Iron and Steel Company which, despite its name, didn't produce any steel, operated from 1870 to 1903 at the peak of the industry's prosperity in West Cumbria. When the Bessemer process was introduced as the first means of producing steel in bulk, the local hematite iron ores were the only ones in the country suitable. While much ore was shipped to other areas from Whitehaven, a great stimulus was given to the local industry. By the 1880s there were twelve ironworks in West Cumbria, three of which had steel-making and rolling plant. These works had no fewer than fifty-four blast furnaces. In addition, there were a number of ancillary firms producing castings, wrought iron and engineering products. Apart from the works at Millom, all were between Whitehaven and Maryport, the district the Cycle Way is just entering, but now it produces neither iron nor steel.

In this part of Whitehaven was the long-defunct William Pit (coal) and there are still signs of it. Most of the coastal pits worked seams several miles out under the sea. North Shore still has one factory, processing fish products - a reminder that the west coast has a small but still flourishing fishing industry. At the time of writing, there are plans to tidy the dereliction around here and develop an industrial estate. Beyond North Shore, the route follows a track between the foot of yellow sandstone cliffs and the railway. These cliffs are unstable, to judge from the netting holding them together in places and several ominously large boulders beside the track, so don't linger too long to savour the view out to sea.

After one and a quarter miles you're back on to the road system, at Parton. The shore here has a reputation for being the point where most flotsam along this coast is ultimately washed up. Poke around; you never know your luck. The place must have been popular among beachcombers in the days of sail, when the frequent onshore winds caused many wrecks (not so popular among sailors presumably). The village had an ironworks, a short-lived venture between 1872 and 1889, and an engineering works. Both have disappeared but the terraced houses built for the ironworkers remain and the slag heaps have been landscaped into recreational parkland. There was also a port, in the eighteenth century, created by the local landowners (this time the Fletchers of Moresby Hall) to export coal. Like the ironworks, however, the project was short-lived. Between Parton and Lowca, on the right of the road, is the site of another Roman fort, one of a line of forts and signal stations that extend from the end of the Hadrian's Wall on the Solway Firth, presumably to prevent it being outflanked from the sea. To see it involves a short though strenuous uphill diversion. (Turn right at the road junction in the valley bottom between Parton and Lowca.)

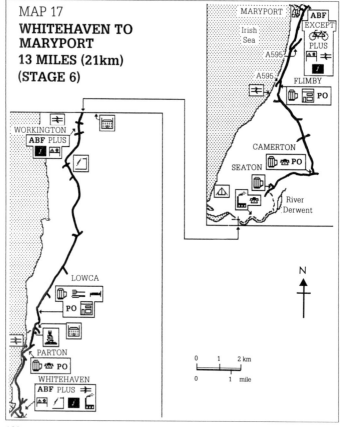

MAP 17

WHITEHAVEN TO MARYPORT

13 MILES (21km)

(STAGE 6)

At the same spot are St Bridget's Church (the Irish connection again) on the remains of the fort, and the late seventeenth-century Moresby Hall (not open to the public but with a splendid façade visible from the road).

Otherwise, turn left, across the valley of the Lowca Beck to the village of that name. Unlike Parton, this was primarily a coalmining settlement, the site of Harrington No. 10 Colliery. It also had an engineering works and a brick works. All three are now defunct, the latter quite recently, so Lowca, like Parton, mainly depends upon the neighbouring towns for employment. Attached to the colliery was a battery of coke ovens but these were a comparatively late addition, built just before the First World War. It might be thought that the local coal, being mined so close to the iron ore and to the iron and steel works, would have fuelled the latter from the start of its expansion. But local coke was not thought suitable; it was imported from Durham using the newly developed railway system. This was at first via Carlisle until a shorter rail route via Keswick, Penrith and Stainmore was opened in 1864. You have already crossed the route of this now-closed railway at Kirkby Stephen and will cross it again in a few miles. A long strike in the Durham coalfield stimulated the development of coking plant in West Cumbria. It was well into the twentieth century before Cumbrian ironmasters accepted local coke.

Beyond Lowca you cross another exposed and treeless ridge with wind-bent hedges, with good views on a clear day: to the Ennerdale Fells, with Pillar the most conspicuous, and across the sea to distant Galloway. The Lake District hills will recede as you go further north and the Scottish ones will become more prominent. Two miles from Lowca, after turning right at a T-junction, the Cycle Way leaves the road once more. It descends to the left, to a disused railway track in an overgrown cutting and then emerges into more open country before entering Workington (Weorc's township"). This is the line of the old Cleator and Workington Junction railway. Created in the 1870s to serve the iron industry, it was meant to combat the monopoly of the London and North Western railway. The latter had bought up most of the local railways, including those that carried local ore to the ironworks around Workington. The new line carried the ore at prices more acceptable to its builders. The

Cycle Way follows this track for five miles, broken only by two short stretches of road. Part is now a concrete cycle track that leads into the centre of Workington and, by way of a tunnel under one of the main streets, into open country beyond.

Workington is older than Whitehaven and, to judge by its name, was originally an Anglian settlement. However, its development as an important port came later than Whitehaven's. Both ports were created by the Lowther family for exporting coal. However, the docks were used increasingly for shipping pig iron and later, when local supplies began to run out, for importing ore. Workington became a shipbuilding town, the ships, as at Whitehaven, being chiefly for the Irish trade. The demand for larger ships virtually killed off that industry in West Cumbria but Workington still has an active port, owned by Cumbria County Council.

Workington was the centre of the iron and steel industry. In the town itself, not including other nearby settlements, there were six ironworks in the 1880s with twenty-one blast furnaces. To provide labour, there was a large immigration of workers from all over the British Isles, supplementing a previous influx of workers to the iron ore and coal mining industries. Now there are neither mines nor iron and steel works, only one establishment of the British Steel Corporation making rails with steel imported from Teesside and a few ancillary industries left over from the boom years. To the west, as you pass through the town, you may see the slag bank at Moss Bay, now landscaped, one of the few memorials to the past. This district is now the largest of the area's Enterprise Zones, where we hope the new Workington is being created.

Lacking the Georgian buildings and layout of Whitehaven, Workington is a typical Victorian industrial town of terraced houses, but it has its attractions. The old part is round Workington Hall, former home of the Curwens, the original holders of the manor. Probably the most famous was John Christian Curwen who married into another local family, the Christians. (Fletcher Christian of *Mutiny on the Bounty* fame, was born in nearby Cockermouth.) John Christian lived in the late eighteenth and early nineteenth centuries and was a radical, an agricultural pioneer and a political opponent of the Lowthers. The Hall is now in ruins, although open to the public during the summer. Its greatest claim to fame is that it was where Mary Queen of Scots spent her first night in England, having landed at Maryport after fleeing from her wrathful fellow countrymen in 1568. Opposite, a road leads to the delightful Portland Square, which many visitors to the town never see. Just up the Cockermouth road is the Helena Thompson Museum which has an excellent local history section dealing with coal and iron ore mining, iron and steel manufacture and shipbuilding. Not far away is the church of St John (1823), with its striking portico.

Beyond the tunnel the Cycle Way goes on to an embankment, which carried an extension of the Cleator and Workington Junction railway. On the right stands a Disney-type building painted bright green. This was the old John Peel brewery, now reduced to a storage function, to the displeasure of many. This open land that you have entered so suddenly from the town centre is alluvial land bordering the River Derwent. As well as an area of allotments where the inhabitants of the local terrace houses can satisfy their horticultural yearnings, it is also the site of the local Easter football matches. These bear little resemblance to conventional football - Association, League or Union - and are played en masse between teams of unlimited numbers called the "Uppies" and the "Downies". These were originally sailors and miners but later the iron and steelworkers muscled in, literally. The game is played with a ball specially made to stand rough handling, the goals about a mile apart, one at the harbour and the other at the walls of Workington Hall. A similar game is played at Ashbourne in Derbyshire where the teams are known as "Uppards" and "Downards". We have heard it muttered that these games have ancient origins and that the "ball" was once the head of an enemy; "Keep you head" might have had other meanings in those days.

The Cycle Way crosses the river by the old railway bridge, but departs to the right from the Workington municipal cycleway (also waymarked) and the line of the Cleator and Workington Junction railway, before it crosses the A596. You are now on another old railway track, once the London and North Western railway's Workington to Cockermouth and Penrith line, but now a pleasant lane along the wide, sheltered valley of the Derwent, with trees growing tall and straight for a change. In half a mile, to the left of the track, is the site of the Barepot ironworks at Seaton, which operated from 1763 until it was dismantled in 1899. Scottish charcoal was used to fuel one blast furnace, which smelted iron intended for wrought iron production. Another produced iron for castings and used local coke suitable for that purpose. The blast for the furnaces was provided by water-powered bellows. A reservoir fed by a canal was built at the rear of the premises to supply the water. These still exist and indeed you will cross the canal within a mile.

Beyond Barepot, the Cycle Way leaves the route of the railway and continues on an unmade road beside the river. It continues round a bend and then strikes away from the river, crossing the canal almost immediately. This is where the railway line to Cockermouth used to cross the canal on a line almost at right angles to that of the Cycle Way. You then climb steeply out of the valley and into Seaton, to rejoin tarred roads. The route only skirts the edge of the village, going through the original part and bypassing the new, which has been considerably built up in the nineteenth and twentieth centuries. Thus, while there are ample facilities in the "new" centre, they are too far away to justify a diversion except in emergency. Leaving Seaton, which is built in an attractive cream-coloured sandstone from the Coal Measures, you head in the direction of Camerton.

There are good views of the Lakeland fells before the road drops to Camerton, originally a mining village. The pub, dated 1625, is called the Black Tom, after Black Tom Curwen whose effigy is in the churchyard (a mile from the village down by the River Derwent). Known as the Champion of the North, to distinguish him from Tom Curwen of Workington (Camerton was in the north diocese (Carlisle), Workington in the diocese of Chester), "Black" referred to the colour of his armour. He died in 1500 and was "a great and fearless warrior" (against the Scots, as you might have guessed). Unfortunately Camerton also has a hill climbing out of it as steep as the one you entered by, so widdershins riders will be in no better shape. The ascent leads to a windy plateau; then down once more, with views across the sea to Criffel and further westward into Galloway. Flimby, on the coast, is at the end of the hilly stretch that began at Sellafield. From here, all the way to Carlisle, you will be on almost level roads. At Flimby, the creamy sandstone is still with us, but there is also a pinkish red one, again from the Coal Measures.

Where the Cycle Way joins the main coast road there are seashore cobbles in garden walls, which we have not seen since Drigg.

In less than one mile our route leaves the A596 by a bridge over the railway, the last you will see until Carlisle, for we are soon about to enter a part of Cumbria that no longer has a rail service. The Cycle Way enters Maryport past an industrial estate run by the local authority. Another, run by English Estates, faces it across the A596. These represent the effort made by national and local government, with varying success, to relieve high unemployment in both the 1930s and the 1980s. Like Barrow-in-Furness, Millom and Whitehaven, Maryport was created as an industrial town by the local land owner, Humphrey Senhouse in this case. However, while Millom and Barrow-in-Furness were nineteenth-century creations, Maryport (like Whitehaven) was founded in the mid eighteenth century. Thus, while all these towns have a crisscross street pattern, the lay-out in Maryport is more reminiscent of Whitehaven than of the other towns. Like Whitehaven, Maryport had a pre-existing village: Ellenfoot, being at the mouth of the River Ellen. In 1750, when the building of the harbour was begun, it was renamed in honour of Humphrey's wife, Mary.

Before entering the town centre, you pass the harbour at the core of the development of the town. Ships used to be built here; and launched sideways because of lack of width in the river. When coal mining began on a significant scale in the eighteenth century there was a need, as at Whitehaven, for a port through which the coal could be exported. At the same time, a blast furnace was erected in Maryport and, although it only lasted until 1783, it was the forerunner of the iron industry in the town. In the boom time of the late nineteenth century, Maryport had two ironworks, with ten blast furnaces, as well as a rolling mill. This stimulated a further need for port facilities and, in the latter half of the last century, two large docks - the Senhouse and the Elizabeth - were built. Maryport, which could take ships up to 6,000 tons, then had a great advantage over Workington, which could only take vessels of up to 2,000 tons. This continued until the opening of the Prince of Wales Dock at Workington in 1927, which caused the collapse of Maryport as a port. Unfortunately that year the second ironworks in Maryport closed, the first and the rolling mill having closed by the end of the

*Maryport Harbour, with the new residential development on the right. The
Senhouse Museum is on the cliffs, just to the right of centre*

nineteenth century. At the same time the local coal mining was
declining with the result that, by the 1930s, the town's economy had
been severely eroded. It has had its moments of relative prosperity
since, but the 1980s brought the closure of many of the firms that had
been brought in to reduce the unemployment of the 1930s.

The docks show the latest attempt to bring the town back to
prosperity. To commemorate the harbour's history as a port a
floating museum of old ships is being set up. A marina is also being
built, and holiday accommodation in a complex that will include a
supermarket. From the harbour, the town centre is entered over a
new bridge. Here, in what was the original part of the town, are the
indoor maritime museum and Tourist Information Office in the
same building. (Collect a leaflet called "Salt making on the Cumbrian
coast", which describes a restored "saltcote" beside the Cycle Way
a few miles ahead.) On the left there's a promenade, overlooking the

sandy beach. This promenade is on a natural terrace between the seashore and a steep slope. Such "raised beaches" are common on the west coast of Scotland but rare in England. The terrace was originally the beach and the steep slope behind was a sea-girt cliff at some period after the melting of the Ice Age glaciers. "But the meltwater from all that ice must have raised the sea level much higher", you may say. True, but the enormous weight of ice had pressed the Earth's crust down. It started rising again after the ice

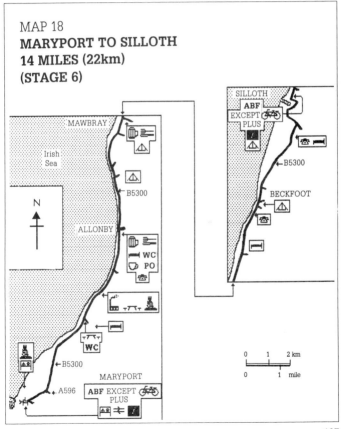

MAP 18
MARYPORT TO SILLOTH
14 MILES (22km)
(STAGE 6)

Fleming Square, Maryport

had gone, but so slowly that it might still be doing it. The raised beach marks a period when the sea level remained static long enough for a beach to develop.

Before leaving Maryport it is worth taking a diversion up the hill behind the raised beach to the Roman fort of Alavna and a new museum. This houses the Roman collection that used to be kept in Netherhall, the now-derelict seat of the Senhouse family, and an exhibition showing the life of the Roman soldier. If you follow the signs to the museum, you will pass through Fleming Square, a large cobbled area bordered by nicely proportioned houses and planted with small trees, reminiscent of a French market place but a rare sight in England.

The Cycle Way returns to the A596 at the parish church (which is of red sandstone, as are the walls of Netherhall Park on the right), then, after passing a school, follows the B5300 between low hedges

The salt pans, on both sides of the road, near to Crosscanonby

and a few wind-bent trees, rejoining the raised beach after a mile. Bracken and gorse flourish between the beach and the road. Believe it or not, a canal was proposed along here in the 1790s, from Maryport almost to Allonby and then inland via Carlisle, all the way to Newcastle. You are now on the line of the Roman road that ran from Alavna up to Hadrian's Wall on the south side of the Solway Firth. Milecastles and turrets were built at regular intervals along this road, which was part of the flank defences of the Wall itself. Once back on the raised beach the road passes a low cliff of reddish clay, the preserved remnant of a drumlin. It would have been eroded by the sea before now if the beach had not been uplifted. Only half a mile along the coast, which is an Area of Outstanding Natural Beauty, there is another exposed drumlin. At the foot stands the re-excavated salt-making site mentioned above, with an explanatory plaque, a viewing point and an adjacent picnic area. At the top is the site of a Roman milecastle.

At Allonby, it is possible to try another sort of saddle

Allonby ("Alleyn's settlement") comes next. This has some red sandstone houses but most are rendered, as a protection against the weather. They are painted in the traditional Cumbrian (and Scottish) way, with the lintels a darker shade than the walls. Some garden walls are of cobbles from the beach. Allonby has been a popular bathing place since the eighteenth century, and in the nineteenth it attracted such well-known novelists as Charles Dickens and Wilkie Collins, whose *The Woman in White* is set partly in Cumberland. Marshall and Walton use the words "genteel isolation", "sedate" and "lethargy" in describing Allonby in *The Lake Counties from 1830 to the Mid-Twentieth Century*. They quote a report made in 1899 by the vicar, who obviously knew his flock: "The summer was not long enough to rook the visitors as they should like to do." The village never benefited from the railway boom of the late nineteenth and early twentieth centuries, but the motor car has helped it regain some of its popularity. If you are tempted to bathe, treat the superb beach with respect. The treacherous tides along this coast can flood in behind you, and patches of quicksand may develop as the tide advances. Have a nice day!

Near Mawbray the dominant marram grass has stabilised the dunes. There is a history of violent storms here, with farmland lost beneath blown sand. Pevsner notes that, north of Mawbray, the sea has swallowed two churches. Newtown, nearby, replaces a village lost to sea or sand in early medieval times. Mawbray itself appears to have been built to house tenants whose land had been overblown by sand. A.J.L.Winchester (*Landscape & Society in Medieval Cumbria*) quotes an order of Lord Dacre in 1555 that the houses were to be built together in one village, "diked and quicksett about and [having] two outgates for their strength and defence against the invasion of the Enemys". "Diked and quicksett" describes the low walls, on which thorn hedges were planted, which we have been seeing along so much of the coast. The "Enemys" were, of course, Scottish raiders, still a menace at that late date. At modern, more peaceful, Mawbray there are still superb cobbled walls.

Heather appears among the gorse and marram grass on the approach to Beckfoot, making this one of the nicest parts of the Cumbrian coast. North of Beckfoot there are dunes on both sides of the road, heathery on the right. Blitterlees, at the entrance to Silloth, is a place-name problem, but a "lea" is temporary grass within an arable rotation. This fits quite well since there is some arable here, making a change from the 100 per cent grass that we have seen along much of the Cycle Way. Freely draining sandy soil, less rainfall, more sunshine and plenty of drying winds make the land dry enough to cultivate in this extremity of the county. (Winters are milder too.)

And so to Silloth ("sea lathe", ie. barn), past the little dock with a big flour mill, and on to yet another gridiron layout, this time with wide streets and open space. This was entirely a railway-company creation of mid-Victorian times, as was Seascale, but with the dual function of port and resort. Silloth, say Marshall and Davies-Shiel (*Industrial Archaeology of the Lake Counties*), has kept its graces. The main street is built only along the landward side. The houses look out over the wide roadway and pine-clad dunes to Criffel in Scotland. This road is made of granite setts, so watch your dentures when riding over them. The railway didn't only bring tourists and stimulate growth of the port, it also carried commuters to work in Carlisle. Now the railway is closed, but the car has replaced it as a means of getting to work, in either Carlisle or the industrial towns of West Cumbria. But Silloth isn't just a retirement, holiday and commuting resort like Grange-over-Sands. The port and its associated industry, together with a couple of industrial estates, give it a better balance of jobs, a wider age-structure and a livelier atmosphere.

Carlisle Castle

Stage 7
Silloth to Carlisle

The Cycle Way continues along the coast road, which after a mile turns away at last from the sandy seashore to Skinburness. Here stood a little market town and port, swept away by the sea in 1301. In more recent times, it became popular as a bathing place and now is an extension of Silloth. A gravel spit, The Grune, extends one mile northeastward and marks the end of the Irish Sea beaches. Eastward lie the tidal mud banks and salt marshes of the Solway Firth. Gravel

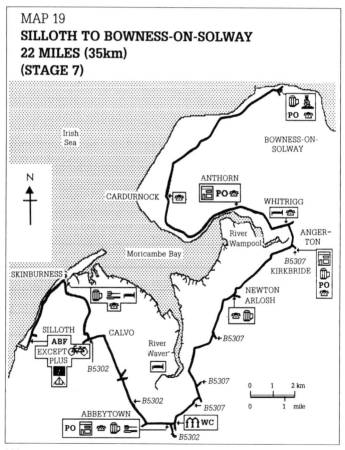

MAP 19
SILLOTH TO BOWNESS-ON-SOLWAY
22 MILES (35km)
(STAGE 7)

spits like The Grune are found where a long beach ends, as for instance where an estuary reaches the sea. If the tides cause a continual movement of sand and gravel in one direction a spit grows out into the estuary. In the end, it becomes unstable, because, as it lengthens, it becomes vulnerable to erosion by tidal currents within the estuary. It is finally breached, usually in some exceptional storm, and the process starts all over again. The lost villages hereabouts are all part of the story and so is the strong current we warned you about at Allonby. A dodgy bit of coast altogether! Readers from Yorkshire might already have noted the resemblance to Spurn Head.

After Skinburness you are again on a salt marsh for the first time since Ravenglass. After crossing the sea dyke (embankment), the road is vulnerable to the highest tides, but only for half a mile. It skirts the perimeter of the former Silloth aerodrome, a Second World War RAF station with some hangars still visible, although it is now an industrial estate. From Sea Dyke End Farm, for one and a half miles to Calvo ("calf hill") on the B5302, you are on a former island made up of glacial boulder clay. After that, it is dead-flat land, once the bed of the estuary of the River Waver. The silty soils here are stoneless, so there are hedges but no stone walls. Many old houses are made of local brick, although some are of stone brought from further afield.

At Kingside Hill the road rises on to a smooth mound of glacial drift that was a small island, just separated from a much bigger ex-island that has Abbeytown perched on its easternmost part. The Abbey after which the village was named was Holm Cultram, a Cistercian foundation dating from 1304. It was as much a local capital, until the Reformation, as was Furness Abbey. Only the nave now remains but at least it is not a roofless ruin like Furness. This is despite the fact that the Abbey was from time to time the target of Scottish raids. Part of the building was preserved as the local church, like Cartmel. Built of red sandstone, it has magnificent pillars and arches, beneath an impressive wooden ceiling. A vast porch, added in 1507, has kept the weather off the Norman doorway that even Pevsner called "glorious."

We are now back in the region where we started - the Border zone. The Solway Firth offered little protection from continual and devastating Scottish raiders. They crossed to Bowness with ease at low tide and life was governed by this menace until the close of the sixteenth century although it was not just one-way traffic. Farming was made difficult and many people on the English side too lived by raiding and petty theft as much as by stock rearing. Neither the English nor the Scots were over-particular as to the nationality of their victims. In fact, blood feuds between neighbouring families seem to have been as common as feuds with families across the Border. Much land was laid waste as a result and, despite its enormous estate, Holm Cultram Abbey was largely dependent on Ireland for corn and provisions in the early 1300s. A 1601 survey said that people "could never keep their goods in safetie, nor scarcelie their own lives". Cultivation was confined to the ex-islands, known as "holms", the flat lands with their high water-table fit only for grazing. In the late fifteenth century the English wool trade, in which the Cistercian monasteries had played an important part, started to decline. This was quickened near the Border because of the raids, in which livestock were driven off in hundreds. Labourers were brought in, under special terms of service, to fight in times of war. Although raiding mostly ceased after the union of the crowns, land enclosures to help new farming techniques and drainage of the flat lands did not make much headway until as late as the nineteenth century.

After the Abbey, the Cycle Way passes the embankment of the old Carlisle-Silloth railway. It then crosses the little River Waver and, half a mile later, leaves the B5307 by an unclassified road that crosses the trackbed of the same railway. From the bridge there is a good view over the salt marshes of the Waver estuary, where the route can again be flooded by spring tides. Despite the openness of the estuary it becomes less windblown as we move further from the Irish Sea. The trees at Salt Cotes Farm (another salt pan name!) are quite straight. This corner of Cumbria may be windy but at least it does not have much snow. At one time during the hard winter of early 1963, this was the only district in the whole of Cumberland, Northumberland and Durham where no snow was lying. It is also less rainy than central Cumbria, where it can be bucketing from leaden clouds when there's often a wedge of brighter sky over the Firth and its shores.

The route returns to the A5307 shortly before it reaches Newton Arlosh. As with Newtown, three miles before Silloth, the village was founded as a replacement for one lost to the sea. In this case the founder was Holm Cultram Abbey and the lost village Skinburness. Newton Arlosh was given a market charter but it did not have enough hinterland to become a market town. Also, as if the depredations of the sea were not enough, the Scottish raids didn't make this the best place to establish a new town. Even the church was built for defence, its tower serving as a pele. Some of the older houses are constructed of local bricks, made from the estuary clay.

From Newton Arlosh, the road runs between drainage ditches across the dead-flat former sea bed. Beyond Angerton House the hedges are growing on earth baulks, probably left when the ditches were dug, thus giving the quickthorn more rooting depth above the water-table. After crossing the old railway again, the Cycle Way touches the north end of the village of Kirkbride, although the Ordnance Survey 1:50,000 map calls this end Angerton. (You will remember another Angerton beside the Duddon estuary in a very similar landscape.) The name Kirkbride, the church of St Bridget, reminds us of the Irish connection again. And wasn't St Patrick himself born in what is now northeast Cumbria? (To be fair he is also claimed by a lot of places both north and south of the Anglo-Scottish border - although not in Ireland.) Kirkbride is a large village, with taller trees then we've seen since Maryport. After the bridge over the River Wampool, the Cycle Way heads back west, beside another salt marsh and then between hedges to Anthorn ("solitary thorn tree"). The new part of this village houses staff of a NATO radio station, the masts of which tower up ahead. The old part has the third and last yellow AA disc. ("London 310$^{1}/_{2}$." We'll not quibble.)

There's a good view from here across Moricambe. This bay is formed by the estuaries of the Rivers Waver and Wampool. Before it silted up, Moricambe was a harbour said to be capable of sheltering fifty ships. The Romans used it, as did Edward I, when he was invading Scotland.

Across the water the trees have grown fairly tall in the old part of Anthorn, despite its nearness to the open sea, but the wide gorse-edged road beyond is treeless and there are no hedges, only wire fences. This is an old airfield, a Fleet Air Arm establishment during the Second World War. The unexpected width of this little-used road suggests that it was once part of the airfield perimeter track. Any trees would have been felled and hedges cleared for safety, so the bleak windswept appearance is probably man-made.

The route now leaves the sea for a while and turns northward to Cardurnock with its garden walls built of seashore cobbles. ("Durnock" is supposed to refer to rounded stones' "Car", meaning a fort, probably refers to one of the chain of Roman fortlets in continuation of Hadrian's Wall.) This is a very quiet stretch, with good views to the Scottish side, dominated by Chapelcross Nuclear Power Station beyond Annan. "Solway sea-washed turf" is dug from the salt marshes here and sold for lawn-making. However, the salt-tolerant grasses will not be able to compete with the ordinary species when the salt has been washed out of the soil by rain. Another, much older, industry on the marshes, naturally enough, is wildfowling, for geese winter here in great numbers.

Tall beeches grow beside the road at Campsfield Farm, proof of the increasing shelter from winds as we leave the open sea. East of North Plain the road is open to the salt marshes seen beyond gorse thickets, but then it rises on to another "island" of glacial boulder clay. There's a nature reserve on the seaward side, extending to a projecting embankment that marks the end of the former viaduct that carried the Solway Junction railway. This left the Carlisle-Silloth line just west of Kirkbride. After crossing the viaduct, it ran into Annan, eventually to join the main Carlisle-Glasgow line. Even when the line closed, the viaduct continued to be of use to raiding Scots, who headed for the pub in Bowness, in the days when the Scottish pubs remained shut on Sundays. The viaduct was demolished before the Second World War and the men of Annan must have had a long, thirsty wait before they got their own pubs open on the Sabbath.

Bowness ("bow-shaped headland"), the northernmost point of the Cycle Way is a huddle of houses. Many are built of an attractive mixture of red sandstone and a dark, slaty rock derived from the Boulder Clay. They were originally borne by glaciers from the Dumfriesshire hills. Bowness stands directly on the site of a Roman fort (Maia), the most westerly one on the line of Hadrian's Wall, which ended here. A plan outside the pub shows the layout of the fort relative to the existing village. This is the most westerly point to be reached by fording the Solway Firth at low tide, which is no doubt why the wall came so far west. In later years, when peace finally came to the Borders, it became a drove route for Scottish cattle to the Wigton cattle fair, from where they went to feed the growing industrial cities of England. In 1767, John Wesley fell foul of the locals here, as he had done eight years earlier at the estuary fords further south, because "the guides were so deeply engaged at

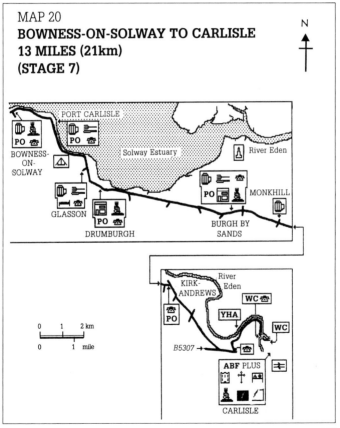

MAP 20
BOWNESS-ON-SOLWAY TO CARLISLE
13 MILES (21km)
(STAGE 7)

a cockfight, that none could be procured to show us over".

Back on the salt marsh once again, the road slips round the outer side of a sea-dyke, becoming flooded by the highest tides each fortnight. Notices again warn you about swift currents and quicksands. The line of Hadrian's Wall and its Vallum, the ditch to the south of it, lie to the right of the present road. From now until Carlisle and beyond, you will be on or near to the line of the Wall. Port Carlisle, the next village with its elegant terrace houses, was the terminus of an eleven-mile canal from Carlisle. It was built in the 1820s and passengers (Liverpool bound) were transferred to ships lying out in the Firth. However, it soon began silting up and was only accessible at high tides. When the port of Silloth, accessible at all states of the tide, was opened, Port Carlisle fell into disuse. The canal was drained in 1853, a little more than thirty years after its construction. A year later it became the trackbed of a railway that connected with the Carlisle-Silloth line at Drumburgh - but that too has disappeared.

A further stretch of tide-washed road is followed by a rise on to rolling boulder clay country. A side road leads off for a quarter of a mile, crossing the ex-canal-cum-ex-railway, to Glasson, a traditional centre of "haaf net" fishing. This is done by men standing in the rising tide water, each holding a net with an eighteen-foot pole. It is a part-time occupation, strictly controlled by a licensing system. Pictures can be seen in the village pub, which bears the unlikely name, in this flat countryside, of "The Highland Laddie". It has been suggested that the name refers to Scottish drovers using the hazardous Solway fords. Just the place for a nerve-steadying pint or dram (for the drovers we mean - they didn't have bikes to fall off) after dodging a capricious tide. Then no doubt they'd have another to set themselves up for the trek through England. After Drumburgh, the site of another Roman fort (Congavata - no signs visible), and with a fine old red sandstone farmhouse, the road crosses a two-mile stretch of salt marsh. It follows a dead straight line beside the embankment of the former railway which here also acts as a sea-dyke. Make the most of this because it is the last coastal section of the Cycle Way, which, since Arnside in the south of the county, has rarely been more than two miles from tidal waters.

Dykesfield is at the end of this straight stretch and nearly into

Burgh by Sands. It marks an abrupt change from flat, bare salt marsh to well-drained undulating farmland, with tall trees and hedges and prosperous-looking villages, reminiscent of Cheshire. Sea-bed clays and silts give way to sands deposited by violent meltwater rivers that streamed out of the Vale of Eden and off the Scottish Border hills at the end of the Ice Age.

Burgh by Sands (pronounced "Bruff") is the largest village you will have seen for many miles and the site of yet another Roman fort. The twelfth-century church, with its massive tower built for defence, was constructed mostly with stone from that great quarry, Hadrian's Wall. A thatched, whitewashed cottage on the north side of the road is what is known as a "clay daubin". It has a base course of massive cobble-stones, which also serves as a foundation for the house's cruck structure. But its two-foot thick walls are made solely of clay, well-rammed (between laths) to make it hard. A layer of straw was added every few inches, to bind it. As it is difficult to make a sharp edge in clay without it crumbling, all original edges are well rounded off. Clay houses were once common all over the Solway plain, where there is no local building stone.

One mile down a lane to the north stands a monument to Edward I, who died on 7 July 1307, at Burgh, aged 68. He was on his way once again to do battle with Robert Bruce, the Scottish king. Edward's tomb at Westminster describes him (in Latin) as the "Hammer of the Scots", although doubtless the Scots had other names for him. His son, Edward II, was a lesser man and was, in due course, soundly hammered himself at Bannockburn. Old campaigns apart, it is worth cycling down this lane, to feel the atmosphere of the lonely marshes. You may see, or at least hear, wild geese; and nowhere else can you cycle out to such a remote spot.

It seems that no poet has captured the spirit of the Solway tides and marshes, in the way that Norman Nicholson did for the Duddon estuary. Yet a poet was born right here, at Burgh by Sands. John Stagg (1770-1823) wrote lively verse about people, their dialect and customs - and he was a fiddler too. Why he never wrote about the estuary is clear from his nickname, The Blind Bard, for he lost his sight in a childhood accident. The Solway Firth is different from Morecambe Bay and the Duddon estuary in another way too. Except to fish, or occasionally to raid or drive cattle, people have not been tempted so much to risk their lives here, for the main fording places on the cross-border route were on the Rivers Eden and Esk *before* they entered the estuary. These fords were comparatively safe, whereas the Morecambe Bay and Duddon crossings were made over wide estuaries, with their quicksands and treacherous tides. Further on, at Monkhill, the village pub, built of local brick, is called "The Drover's Rest", indicating another Solway-side drove road. There's brickwork again at Kirkandrews because the bedrock around Carlisle, under glacial clays and sands, is a weak, soft mudstone, useless for building. Thus most of Carlisle is built of brick. All stone has had to be brought in from further afield, except that which Hadrian thoughtfully provided.

The last fields before the city are bounded by neat hedges on earth banks, after which the Cycle Way becomes an urban road that, in half a mile, joins the busier B5307 that you left at Kirkbride. A quarter of a mile further on, at a phone box, turn northward (left) and soon enter a lane between a new housing estate and a rugby field. Then bear half right across a cleared industrial area towards a large electricity pylon, until a waymark sign is seen on the left. This was originally the area crossed by the canal, which terminated nearby. Later there were two railway junctions here and an engine shed. The line to Silloth, with a connection to Port Carlisle, crossed this area, as well as the North British railway line that went eventually to Edinburgh. Now it mainly seems to be used by people exercising dogs and by small boys getting up to mischief.

The Cycle Way can't avoid plunging down a flight of wooden steps here, to the banks of the river Eden, passing beneath an elegantly curved railway bridge that carried the former North British line on its way to Scotland. If you're hoping to nip across here to the Youth Hostel, you will be disappointed - the bridge is blocked. The Cycle Way continues upstream, past more recent industrial archaeology in the form of a disused power station. The area is now an industrial estate and the part nearest the route is a gas bottling plant. It gets prettier after this, with trees lining the river. After going beneath the still-existing London-Glasgow railway (which means that you are once more near a railway station), curve round a sports field and recreational centre. Here, at the bridge over the River Caldew, you have reached the place where we began. And that's it! You've finished. Rather an anticlimax perhaps, after the ever-changing Cycle Way - the hills and dales, villages and towns, marshes estuaries and dunes.

The choice of direction is yours now, depending upon whether you are starting, finishing (permanently, just for the night or for a few hours only) or bashing straight on through. The finishers should head south in the direction of the castle and the town centre. The bashers-on, plus those who have found the Cycle Way habit-forming and wish to do a second circuit should carry on east or even turn round and do it widdershins. One thing you could do is something that very few Cumbrians seem to be able to do: break through the psychological barrier of Hadrian's Wall to discover that the county continues northward for twenty more miles, with Rockcliffe, Solway Moss, the lush Esk valley, Kershope Forest, the remote valleys of the White Lyne and Black Lyne, pele towers and Bewcastle Cross, all waiting to be explored. And beyond that, you've the whole of Scotland, beginning perhaps with a pilgrimage to Keir Mill, near Dumfries, where the village blacksmith, Kirkpatrick Macmillan (otherwise known as Mad Pate) invented and built the first bicycle, in 1840. Be careful, or you may never get home at all.

But see Carlisle first, the only city in England with a fully Celtic name (originally Caer Luel - fort named after Luel, possibly a Celtic god), developed as a Roman centre at the point where Hadrian's Wall crossed the River Eden. In fact, there were two Roman forts (Luguvalium and Patriana), on either side of the river, but they were not in use at the same time. (Tullie House Museum has one of the best Roman collections in the country. It is also a first-class heritage centre, telling the history of the city and the surrounding countryside.) Later, Carlisle became a Norman stronghold guarding the Western Marches of the border against the Scots (although in fact the city, like most of the rest of Cumbria, was twice under Scottish rule and was claimed as being part of the kingdom of Scotland for a long time afterwards).

The massive castle contains an exhibition that describes its history. It also holds the museum of the Border Regiment (now, after merger, the King's Own Border Regiment). With other museums at the cathedral and guildhall, history buffs won't be short of things to do. Carlisle was also the centre of an episcopal see, which is evident from the cathedral and, although smaller than many towns, its status as a city. Another function of the city was as capital of Cumberland and, since 1974, of Cumbria. This function is represented by the Tudor guildhall and the more recent Courts, which house both the Law Courts and the headquarters of Cumbria County Council. The oldest part is compact and easily explored: a lozenge shape extending only a quarter of a mile southward from the castle. As well as most of the buildings already mentioned, it contains the delightful Cathedral Close, vestiges of the city walls and a medieval tithe barn. The centre of a large agricultural lowland, embracing both kingdoms, the city therefore became the main agricultural, commercial and industrial centre. Much of its industry is related to food and drink. Even industries, past and present, such as textiles, general engineering and leather goods reflect its market town origins. One exception is the branch factory of an Italian tyre firm. In the railway age Carlisle became the centre of a network of lines, many now disused, as you have seen. Finally, it is the main shopping area of the region, despite the competition of Tyneside shopping centres. The prize-winning indoor shopping centre of The Lanes together with the covered market are an added attraction. On a market day especially, you'll hear accents not only of North and West Cumbria, the Lake District and the upper Tyne valley, but of Dumfriesshire too.

So, those finishing the route here should find plenty to occupy them before they head for home. Our congratulations to you. To those for whom Carlisle is just another landmark on the Cycle Way we wish good luck. Don't keep your noses too closely to the wheel. We hope we've shown you that it's worthwhile looking about you.

* * *

BOOKS CONSULTED

Backhouse, Janet. *The Lindisfarne Gospels.* Phaidon Press, London 1981

Chancellor, F.B. *Around Eden.* Whitehead, Appleby 1954

Clare, Tom. *Archaeological Sites of the Lake District.* Moorland Publishing, Ashbourne 1981

Cumberland & Westmorland Antiquarian & Archaeological Society. Transactions

English Place-Names Society. County Volumes

Fraser, George Macdonald. *The Steel Bonnets.* 2nd edn Pan Books, London 1974

Hindle, Brian Paul. *Roads & Trackways of the Lake District.* Moorland Publishing, Ashbourne 1984

Hunt, Irvine. *The Lakeland Pedlar.* 2nd edn Rusland Press, Ulverston 1977

Jowett, Alan. *Jowett's Railway Atlas of Great Britain & Ireland.* Patrick Stephens Ltd, Wellingborough 1989

Lancaster, J.Y. and D.R.Wattleworth. *The Iron and Steel Industry of West Cumberland.* British Steel Corporation 1977

Macleod, Innes (editor). *Sailing on Horseback. William Daniell and Richard Ayton in Cumbria and Dumfries and Galloway.* T.C.Farries & Co. Ltd, Dumfries 1988

Manley, Gordon. 'The Climate of Cumberland and Westmorland' in *The Report of the Land Utilisation Survey of Britain.* Geographical Publications. 1943

Marshall, J.D. *Portrait of Cumbria.* Robert Hale Ltd, London 1981

Marshall, J.D. and Michael Davies-Shiel. *Industrial Archaeology of the Lake Counties.* 2nd edn Michael Moon, Beckermet 1977.

Marshall, J.D. and Walton, J.K. *The Lake Counties from 1830 to the Mid-Twentieth century.* Manchester University Press 1981

Millward, Roy and Adrian Robinson. *The Lake District.* Eyre Methuen. London 1974

Morris, C. (editor). *The Illustrated Journeys of Celia Fiennes.* Macdonald, London 1984

Nicholson, Norman. *Rock Face.* Faber & Faber, London 1948

Parker, C.A. *The Gosforth District.* Titus Wilson, Kendal 1904

Pevsner, Nikolaus. *The Buildings of England.* Penguin, Harmondsworth. Cumberland and Westmorland 1967. North Lancashire 1969

Robinson, Peter W. *Railways of Cumbria.* Dalesman, Clapham 1980

Smith, Kenneth. *Cumbrian Villages.* Robert Hale, London 1973

Thompson, Mary M. *Mallerstang: a Westmorland Dale.* Whitehead, Appleby 1965

Versey, M.C. *Geology of the Appleby District.* Whitehead, Appleby 1941

Wilson, J.Oliver. *Birds of Westmorland & the Northern Pennines.* Hutchinson, London 1933

Winchester, A.J.L. *Landscape & Society in Medieval Cumbria.* John Donald, Edinburgh 1987

*   *   *

CYCLE SHOPS & CYCLE HIRE

ARNSIDE

South Cumbria Cycle Hire, Sunny Cote, Silverdale Rd. 0524-762065 (Repairs, Hire)

BARROW-IN-FURNESS

Blackshaws Ltd, 80 Dalton Rd. 0229-820111 (Spares, Repairs)

Grange Cycles, 275-277 Rawlinson St. 0229-811049 (Spares, Repairs)

J R Cycles, 27 Risedale Rd. 0229-838922 (Spares, Repairs)

Top Mark Mountain Bikes, 108 Greengate St. 0229-824740 (Spares, Repairs)

BRAMPTON

C R Charlton, 3 Shepherds Lane. 06977-3154 (Spares, Repairs)

Talkin Tarn Country Park. 06977-3129 (Hire)

BROUGHTON-IN-FURNESS

Mountain Centre Sports Equipment, Brade St & Market St. 0229-716461 (Spares, Repairs)

CARLISLE
>Border Cycles Ltd, 133 Lowther St. 0228-36872 (Spares, Repairs)
>Palace Cycle Stores, 122 Botchergate. 0228-23142 (Spares, Repairs)
>Whiteheads, 104/108 Botchergate. 0228-26890 (Spares, Repairs)

GRANGE-OVER-SANDS
>Grange Cycles, 2 Woodside, Main St. 05395-33333 (Spares, Repairs)

KIRKBY STEPHEN
>H.S.Robinson, 2 Market St. 07683-71519 (Spares, Repairs, Hire)

MILLOM
>Charles McIntosh, 63 Queen St. 0229-772294 (Spares, Repairs)

SEDBERGH
>Sedbergh Cycles, Howgill Lane. 05396-21000 (Spares, Repairs, Hire)

ULVERSTON
>North West Cycle Sport, 52 Hart St. 0229-54417 (Spares, Repairs)
>D & M Polkinghorn, Upper Brook St. Garage. 0229-52765 (Spares, Repairs)

WHITEHAVEN
>Mark Taylor, King St. 0946-692252 (Spares, Repairs)

WORKINGTON
>Mark Taylor, 4 Murray Rd. 0900-603280 (Spares, Repairs)
>New Bike Shop, Market Place. 0900-603337 (Spares, Repairs)
>Traffic Lights Bike Shop, 35 Washington St. 0900-603283 (Spares, Repairs)

*   *   *

IF YOU LIKE ADVENTUROUS ACTIVITIES ON MOUNTAINS OR HILLS YOU WILL ENJOY READING:

CLIMBER

AND HILLWALKER

MOUNTAINEERING/HILLWALKING/TREKKING ROCK CLIMBING/SCRAMBLING IN BRITAIN AND ABROAD

AVAILABLE FROM NEWSAGENTS, OUTDOOR EQUIPMENT SHOPS, OR BY SUBSCRIPTION (6-12 MONTHS) FROM OUTRAM MAGAZINES, THE PLAZA TOWER, EAST KILBRIDE, GLASGOW G74 1LW

THE WALKERS' MAGAZINE

the great OUTDOORS

COMPULSIVE MONTHLY READING FOR ANYONE INTERESTED IN WALKING

AVAILABLE FROM NEWSAGENTS, OUTDOOR EQUIPMENT SHOPS, OR BY SUBSCRIPTION (6-12 MONTHS) FROM OUTRAM MAGAZINES, THE PLAZA TOWER, EAST KILBRIDE, GLASGOW G74 1LW

Printed by
Carnmor Print & Design, London Road, Preston